Heaven

Heaven

by
John MacArthur, Jr.

MOODY PRESS
CHICAGO

Library of Congress Cataloging in Publication Data

MacArthur, John, 1939-
    Heaven / by John MacArthur, Jr.
      p.   cm. — (John MacArthur's Bible studies)
    Includes indexes.
    ISBN 0-8024-5383-X
    1. Heaven—Biblical teaching.   2. Bible—Criticism,
interpretation, etc. I. Title. II. Series: MacArthur, John, 1939-
Bible studies.
    BS680.H42M33   1988
    236'.24—dc19   88-28320
                                                CIP

© 1988 by
JOHN F. MACARTHUR, JR.

Scripture quotations, unless noted otherwise, are taken from the *New American Standard Bible,* © 1960, 1962, 1963, 1968, 1971, 1972, 1973, 1975, and 1977 by The Lockman Foundation. Used by permission.

Moody Press, a ministry of the Moody Bible Institute, is designed for education, evangelization, and edification. If we may assist you in knowing more about Christ and the Christian life, please write us without obligation: Moody Press, c/o MLM, Chicago, Illinois 60610.

ISBN: 0-8024-5383-X

1 2 3 4 5 6 7 8 Printing/LC/Year 93 92 91 90 89 88

Printed in the United States of America

Contents

These Bible studies are taken from messages delivered by Pastor-Teacher John MacArthur, Jr., at Grace Community Church in Panorama City, California. The recorded messages themselves may be purchased as a series or individually. Please request the current price list by writing to:

WORD OF GRACE COMMUNICATIONS
P.O. Box 4000
Panorama City, CA 91412

Or call the following toll-free number:
1-800-55-GRACE

1
Looking Toward Heaven—Part 1
What Heaven Is

Outline

Introduction
A. The Preciousness of Heaven
B. The Priority of Heaven
  1. Explained
  2. Exemplified
    a) Paul's situation
    b) Paul's shell
      (1) The decay of the earthly body
      (2) The anticipation of an eternal body
    c) Paul's strategy

Lesson
I. What Heaven Is
A. A Place
  1. The atmospheric heaven
  2. The planetary heaven
  3. The divine heaven
    a) In the Old Testament
    b) In the New Testament
      (1) Revelation
      (2) Matthew
      (3) John
B. A Sphere
  1. Explained
  2. Examined

Conclusion

Introduction

We live in a time when credit cards allow us to buy what we cannot afford, go where we could not go, and do what would otherwise be impossible for us. Sometimes we allow our indebtedness to increase until we cannot meet our obligations—and serious difficulties result. The credit problem is symptomatic of an attitude that says, "I want what I want when I want it!" The mind-set of our age is against postponing anything. We prefer instant gratification, gladly sacrificing the future on the altar of the immediate.

Unfortunately, the church has fallen prey to such materialistic indulgence. Rather than setting their affections on things above (Col. 3:1), many Christians are attached to the earth. Rather than laying up treasure in heaven, they have dedicated themselves to accumulating treasure on earth. Certain television and radio ministries, preaching a prosperity gospel, tell people that Jesus wants them to be healthy, wealthy, and successful. Such teaching is extremely popular, because it caters to the desire in people to have everything in this life. Because the church doesn't always have heaven on its mind, sometimes it is indulgent, self-centered, and weak. Sometimes its present comfort consumes its thoughts, and it entertains only passing thoughts of heaven.

A. The Preciousness of Heaven

In reality, everything that is precious to us as Christians is in heaven.

1. Our Father

In Matthew 6:9 Jesus says, "Pray, then, in this way: 'Our Father who art in heaven, hallowed be Thy name.' " Our Father, who is the source of everything, is in heaven.

2. Our Savior

Hebrews 9:24 says, "Christ did not enter a holy place made with hands, a mere copy of the true one, but into heaven itself, now to appear in the presence of God for us." Our Savior is also in heaven.

3. Our brothers and sisters in Christ

   Hebrews 12:23 says, "To the general assembly and church of the first-born who are enrolled in heaven, and to God, the Judge of all, and to the spirits of righteous men made perfect." Our brothers and sisters in the faith are in heaven. Every Old and New Testament believer who has died is there.

4. Our names

   In Luke 10:20 Christ tells His disciples, who were casting out demons, "Do not rejoice in this, that the spirits are subject to you, but rejoice that your names are recorded in heaven." By saying that our names are written in heaven, Christ assures us that we have a title deed to property there.

5. Our inheritance

   First Peter 1:3-4 says, "Blessed be the God and Father of our Lord Jesus Christ, who according to His great mercy has caused us to be born again to a living hope through the resurrection of Jesus Christ from the dead, to obtain an inheritance which is imperishable and undefiled and will not fade away, reserved in heaven for you." Our eternal inheritance—all the riches of God's glory and grace—is in heaven.

6. Our citizenship

   In Philippians 3:20 Paul observes that "our citizenship is in heaven." We are citizens; we belong there.

7. Our eternal reward

   In Matthew 5:12 Jesus says we are to consider ourselves blessed when others persecute us because our reward is in heaven.

8. Our Master

   In Ephesians 6:9 Paul reminds us that our Master is in heaven.

9. Our treasure

In Matthew 6:19-21 Jesus says that the only treasure we will possess throughout eternity is in heaven.

Heaven is our home. Christians are strangers, pilgrims, and aliens in this world.

B. The Priority of Heaven

1. Explained

Everything we love, everything we value, everything eternal is in heaven. Nevertheless, the church in this century has tended to be self-indulgent, proof that many Christians have lost their heavenly perspective. Too many people do not want to go to heaven until they have enjoyed all that the world can offer. Only when all earthly pursuits are exhausted, or when age and sickness hamper their enjoyment, are they ready for heaven. "Please God," they pray, "don't take me to heaven yet; I haven't been to Hawaii!" or, "I haven't gotten my new car or house."

First John 2 says, "If anyone loves the world, the love of the Father is not in him. . . . The world is passing away" (vv. 15, 17). Many people who claim to love Christ love the world so much that they can't possibly be citizens of heaven. As the old spiritual says, everybody talking about heaven ain't going there! But everyone going to heaven isn't talking about it, either. The hope of heaven should fill us with a joy of anticipation that loosens us from this transitory world. We can easily become so attached to the world that we spend our energy consuming things that will perish rather than accumulating treasure in heaven. Some people believe heaven is an imaginary place. Others believe heaven is a state of mind, a projection of all that is good in humanity. Some believe it is the immortality of truth and beauty. But the Bible says that heaven is a place, the eventual dwelling of all who love God. We will live there forever in complete perfection and glory.

2. Exemplified

a) Paul's situation

When Paul wrote 2 Corinthians, he was facing overwhelming persecution. In 4:8-10 he says, "We are afflicted in every way, but not crushed; perplexed, but not despairing; persecuted, but not forsaken; struck down, but not destroyed; always carrying about in the body the dying of Jesus, that the life of Jesus also may be manifested in our body." In verses 16-17 he says, "We do not lose heart, but though our outer man is decaying, yet our inner man is being renewed day by day. For momentary, light affliction is producing for us an eternal weight of glory far beyond all comparison." Paul was saying that whatever we endure in this life cannot be compared with the glory it is producing in the life to come. When the mother of James and John asked Christ if He would allow her sons to sit on His left and right in the kingdom, Christ said that decision was the Father's, but He implied that the Father would give the honor to the one who suffered most here for His name (Matt. 20:21-23). The suffering we endure on earth will be compensated for in eternity.

b) Paul's shell

Paul continued, "We look not at the things which are seen, but at the things which are not seen; for the things which are seen are temporal, but the things which are not seen are eternal. For we know that if the earthly tent which is our house is torn down, we have a building from God, a house not made with hands, eternal in the heavens" (2 Cor. 4:18–5:1).

(1) The decay of the earthly body

Our earthly tent is being torn down. I remember reading that when someone asked John Quincy Adams how he was doing, Adams replied something to the effect of, "John Quincy Adams is well, sir, very well. The house in which he has been living is dilapidated and old, and he has received word from its Maker that he must vacate soon. But John Quincy Adams is well, sir, very well." In the same way our earthly tent is being torn down. But when it's gone, we'll have a building from God, eternal in the heavens. Second Corinthians 5:2 says of our earthly bodies, "Indeed in this house we groan." We groan because of the infirmities of the flesh and the sin that permeates it. We groan because we cannot be what we long to be. We are debilitated in these bodies, so we groan with the rest of creation, waiting "eagerly for the revealing of the sons of God" (Rom. 8:19). We long to be clothed with a heavenly body.

(2) The anticipation of an eternal body

In 2 Corinthians 5:2-4 Paul continues, "We groan, longing to be clothed with our dwelling from heaven; inasmuch as we, having put it on, shall not be found naked. For indeed while we are in this tent, we groan, being burdened, because we do not want to be unclothed, but to be clothed, in order that what is mortal may be swallowed up by life." Although in this body we groan because we are burdened by sin, sickness, sorrow, and death, we do not want to be unclothed. We want both our spirits and our bodies to enter the presence of God. Paul yearned for heaven and his eternal body.

Verse 5 says, "He who prepared us for this very purpose is God, who gave to us the Spirit as a pledge." The Greek word translated "pledge" is *arrabōn*, the same word Paul uses in Ephesians 1:14 to refer to the Holy Spirit. In modern Greek a form of *arrabōn* refers to an engagement ring. In New Testament times the word referred to a down payment or first installment—earnest money. Therefore, the Holy Spirit is the pledge of the new body we will have in the glories of heaven.

12

c) Paul's strategy

In verses 6-8 Paul mentions the practical results of his teaching in the previous verses: "Therefore, being always of good courage, and knowing that while we are at home in the body we are absent from the Lord—for we walk by faith, not by sight—we are of good courage, I say, and prefer rather to be absent from the body and to be at home with the Lord." Do those verses express the deepest desire of your heart? We tend to hold tightly to this world because it's all we know. Because we experience meaningful relationships here, we become captive to this life. But notice that Paul said "at home with the Lord." We are at home only when we're with the Lord. That's where we belong.

As we examine what the Bible teaches about heaven, we should long to be clothed with our heavenly form. We should look forward to being absent from the body and present with the Lord. We should become more preoccupied with the glories of eternity rather than the afflictions of today. We need to spend our energy accumulating heavenly treasures rather than amassing treasures here that are ultimately meaningless. After a rich person died, someone asked one of his friends how much he left. The friend answered, "All of it." And that's exactly what each of us will leave.

Lesson

I. WHAT HEAVEN IS

The Bible refers to heaven approximately 550 times. The Hebrew word translated "heaven" (*shamayim*) is plural and literally means "the heights." The Greek word translated "heaven" is *ouranos*, which inspired the name of the planet Uranus. The word refers to that which is raised up or lofty.

13

A. A Place

Both those words are used to refer to three different places. In 2 Corinthians 12:2 Paul says, "Such a man [probably a reference to himself] was caught up to the *third* heaven" (emphasis added). That clearly demonstrates that there are three heavens.

1. The atmospheric heaven

Sometimes when the Bible speaks of heaven, it refers to the region called the troposphere—the atmosphere around the earth, the air we breathe. For example, Isaiah 55:9 says, "As the heavens are higher than the earth, so are My ways higher than your ways, and My thoughts than your thoughts. For as the rain and the snow come down from heaven . . ." Here the word *heaven* refers to the atmosphere, which is where the hydrological cycle occurs. Psalm 147:8 says that God "covers the heavens with clouds." That is the first heaven.

2. The planetary heaven

The second heaven contains the stars, moons, and planets. Scripture also mentions this heaven. For example, Genesis 1 says, "God said, Let there be lights in the expanse of the heavens. . . . God made the two great lights, the greater light to govern the day, and the lesser light to govern the night; He made the stars also. And God placed them in the expanse of the heavens to give light on the earth" (vv. 14, 16-17). That's the second heaven.

3. The divine heaven

The third heaven is the place where God dwells with His holy angels and believers who have died.

How Can an Omnipresent God Live in Heaven?

In 1 Kings 8:27 Solomon prays, "Heaven and the highest heaven [lit., "heaven of heavens"] cannot contain Thee, how much less

14

this house which I have built!" In a sense the heaven of heavens cannot contain God, yet in another sense it is His dwelling place. A simple illustration may help to clarify how both can be true: I live in a house, but that house cannot contain me. My house doesn't contain me bodily at all times, and it certainly can't contain the effect of my life—my influence. Although that is an imperfect illustration, it expresses how God can dwell in heaven but at the same time not be limited or contained by it.

a) In the Old Testament

Isaiah 57:15 says, "Thus says the high and exalted One who lives forever, whose name is Holy, I dwell on a high and holy place." God has a real dwelling place. Isaiah 63:15 identifies that place: "Look down from heaven, and see from Thy holy and glorious habitation." Psalm 33:13-14 says, "The Lord looks from heaven; He sees all the sons of men; from His dwelling place He looks out." There is a place where God dwells, and that place is called heaven. It's the heaven of heavens, the third heaven. Psalm 102:19 says, "He looked down from His holy height; from heaven the Lord gazed upon the earth."

b) In the New Testament

(1) Revelation

Revelation 3:12 says, "He who overcomes, I will make him a pillar in the temple of My God, and he will not go out from it anymore; and I will write upon him the name of My God, and the name of the city of My God, the new Jerusalem, which comes down out of heaven from My God." John describes the city as descending out of heaven at God's command.

(2) Matthew

Christ repeatedly stressed that the Father is in heaven. In Matthew 5:16 He says, "Let your light shine before men in such a way that they may see

15

your good works, and glorify your Father who is in heaven." In verse 34 He says, "Make no oath at all, either by heaven, for it is the throne of God." Verse 45 says, "That you may be the sons of your Father who is in heaven." Matthew 6:1 says, "Beware of practicing your righteousness before men to be noticed by them; otherwise you have no reward with your Father who is in heaven." In verse 9 Christ says, "Pray, then, in this way: 'Our Father who art in heaven.' " Matthew 7:11 says, "If you then, being evil, know how to give good gifts to your children, how much more shall your Father who is in heaven give what is good to those who ask Him!" Verse 21 says, "Not everyone who says to me, 'Lord, Lord,' will enter the kingdom of heaven; but he who does the will of My Father who is in heaven." Matthew 10:32-33 says, "Everyone therefore who shall confess Me before men, I will also confess him before My Father who is in heaven. But whosoever shall deny Me before men, I will also deny him before My Father who is in heaven."

Matthew 12:50 says, "Whoever does the will of My Father who is in heaven, he is My brother and sister and mother." In Matthew 16:17 Jesus says to Peter, "Blessed are you, Simon Barjona, because flesh and blood did not reveal this to you, but My Father who is in heaven." Matthew 18:10 says, "Do not despise one of these little ones [believers], for I say unto you, that their angels in heaven continually behold the face of My Father who is in heaven." Verse 14 says, "It is not the will of your Father who is in heaven that one of these little ones perish." Verse 19 says, "If two of you agree on earth about anything that they may ask, it shall be done for them by My Father who is in heaven." In verse 35 Christ says, "So shall My heavenly Father also do to you."

(3) John

In John 6 Jesus says, "The bread of God is that which comes down out of heaven, and gives life

16

to the world" (v. 33). Again Jesus linked God and heaven. In verse 38 Christ says, "I have come down from heaven." In verses 41-42 He says, "I am the bread that came down out of heaven. . . . I have come down out of heaven." In verses 50-51 He says, "This is the bread which comes down out of heaven, so that one may eat of it and not die. I am the living bread that came down out of heaven." Verse 58 says, "This is the bread which came down out of heaven."

Heaven is not a figment of imagination, a feeling, or an emotion—it's a place, God's place.

A Key to Interpreting the New Testament

Heaven was connected with God so much that it became a synonym for God Himself. That usage was common in the New Testament. In Matthew 23:22 Jesus says, "He who swears by heaven, swears both by the throne of God and by Him who sits upon it." Heaven in that verse is synonymous with God. You can refer either to heaven or to God and mean both. In Luke 15:7 Christ says that "there will be . . . joy in heaven over one sinner who repents." The following parables, including that of the prodigal son, show that the "joy in heaven" refers to joy in the heart of God. In fact, the prodigal son, rehearsing what he would say to his Father, said, "I will get up and go to my father, and will say to him, 'Father, I have sinned against heaven' " (Luke 15:18). That meant the same thing as sinning against God.

When the writers of Scripture speak of the kingdom of heaven, they are actually referring to the kingdom of God. Particularly during the Intertestamental Period, the four hundred years between the events of the Old Testament and the New, the Jewish people developed a fear of using God's name. They didn't use the covenant name of God (Yahweh or Jehovah) because they believed it was too holy. As a result, they substituted other words for the name of God, and "heaven" became a common substitute. By New Testament times that practice was so ingrained that the Jewish people understood any reference to the kingdom of heaven as a reference to the kingdom of God.

B. A Sphere

1. Explained

In Ephesians 1:3 the apostle Paul says, "Blessed be the God and Father of our Lord Jesus Christ, who has blessed us with every spiritual blessing in the heavenly places [heavenlies] in Christ." Notice that the verb tense indicates that the blessing occurred in the past. Ephesians 2:4-6 says, "God, being rich in mercy . . . even when we were dead in our transgressions, made us alive together with Christ (by grace you have been saved), and raised [past tense] us up with Him, and seated [past tense] us with Him in the heavenly places, in Christ Jesus." Although we aren't yet in heaven, we are in the heavenlies. Heaven is where God lives and rules. We aren't in the place called heaven, but we are under the dominion of the King of heaven, so we are living in the heavenlies.

Christ preached that the kingdom of heaven or kingdom of God was at hand. He called people to enter that kingdom, to be saved, and to inherit eternal life. Those three expressions all point to one experience: salvation. Whenever someone believes in Christ, he enters the kingdom of God—he comes under God's rule, not in heaven but in the heavenlies. Although we don't yet live in heaven, we do live in the heavenlies and should therefore be preoccupied with heavenly things. Our new life in Christ is in the heavenlies—it is under the rule and dominion of God.

2. Examined

Heaven will be a new community of holiness and fellowship with God, a place of joy, peace, love, and fulfillment. But we experience that partially even now. The Holy Spirit is producing in us the fruit of "love, joy, peace, patience, kindness, goodness, faithfulness, gentleness, self-control" (Gal. 5:22-23). Those traits characterize heaven. That's what Fanny Crosby meant by "a foretaste of glory divine" in her hymn "Blessed Assurance." We are tasting now what we will enjoy in heaven. We have the life of God in us and the rule of God over us. We know joy, peace, love, goodness, and blessing. We have become part of a new family, a new community. We have left the kingdom of darkness for the kingdom of light. We are no longer under the dominion of Satan but the dominion of God in Christ. Second Corinthians 5:17 says, "If any man is in Christ, he is a new creature; the old things passed away; behold, new things have come." We are new creations.

We are members of a new family. Rather than remaining the children of Satan, we have become the children of God. Galatians 4:26 says that Jerusalem is our mother, referring not to the earthly Jerusalem, but to the Jerusalem where God rules. We have a new citizenship (Phil. 3:20), new affections (Col. 3:1), and a new storehouse where we are to store our treasures (Matt. 6:19-20).

Conclusion

Heaven is an actual place, but it is also a sphere in this world where God rules. The best of our spiritual experiences here is only a taste of heaven. Our highest spiritual heights, profoundest depths, and greatest spiritual blessings will be normal in heaven. As we live now in the heavenlies, we are merely tasting the glories of the life to come. To us heaven is now a sphere where we live under God's rule and His Spirit's blessing. One day it will also be a place where we will walk in our glorified bodies. In John 17 Christ prays, "Father, I desire that they also, whom Thou hast given Me, be with Me where I am, in order that they may behold My glory" (v. 24). In John 14:1-3 Christ says to His disciples, "Let not your heart be troubled; believe in God, believe also in Me. In My Father's house are many dwelling places; if it were not so, I would have told you; for I go to prepare a place for you. And if I go and prepare a place for you, I will come again, and receive you to Myself; that where I am, there you may be also." Jesus is preparing a place where we will live in a glorified, physical form similar to that of the resurrected body of Christ. He walked, ate, and sang, but He also ascended through space into the third heaven.

We are longing for "the city which has foundations, whose architect and builder is God" (Heb. 11:10). In ancient times a city was a place of safety and refuge. The nomadic people of those times were especially vulnerable to robbers, thieves, and the elements. Imagine after many weeks or even months of such wandering how refreshing it was to enter the protection of a walled city. Every Christian needs to see himself as a pilgrim, wandering through this world, looking for "the city . . . whose architect and builder is God"—an actual place where we will live with Christ. We will be with Him, just as the disciples were with Him after His resurrection. Like Thomas, we will touch Him. We will sit with Him and sing with Him. The joy we have of walking with Christ and knowing that the Spirit lives within us is the pledge that one day we will live in heaven.

There Is No Purgatory

If you are a Christian, the moment you leave this life you go to heaven. The Bible doesn't teach what the medieval theologians referred to as *limbus patrum*, or limbo. There is no purgatory. Paul said he preferred "to be absent from the body and to be at home with the Lord" (2 Cor. 5:8). He said he desired "to depart and be with Christ" (Phil. 1:23).

When we consider that Christ prayed that all who know Him would spend eternity with Him (John 17:24), our hearts should overflow with gratitude. We need to have the heart of Paul— yearning to to be clothed with our heavenly form and to exchange this transient world for eternal joy.

Focusing on the Facts

1. What things make heaven precious to us (see pp. 8-10)?
2. Explain 2 Corinthians 4:17 (see p. 11).
3. Why does Paul say, "In this house we groan" (see p. 12)?
4. What does *arrabōn* mean? What insight does its meaning give to 2 Corinthians 5:5 (see p. 12)?
5. How often does the Bible refer to heaven? What are the Greek and Hebrew words translated "heaven," and what do they mean (see p. 13)?
6. What passage clearly illustrates that there are three heavens? Explain (see p. 14).

7. The Bible refers to what three heavens (see p. 14)?
8. Explain how an omnipresent God can live in heaven (see pp. 14-15).
9. List some passages in the gospels that state God is in heaven (see pp. 15-17).
10. Why did the New Testament writers occasionally substitute "heaven" for God's name? How does that practice affect the interpretation of the phrase "kingdom of heaven" (see p. 17)?
11. What do entering the kingdom, being saved, and inheriting eternal life have in common (see p. 18)?
12. Whenever someone _____ in _____ , he enters the kingdom of God. Explain (see p. 18).
13. Heaven is an actual _____ , but it is also a _____ in this world where God rules (see p. 19).
14. Explain the imagery and significance of Hebrews 11:10 (see pp. 19-20).
15. What passages make clear that there is no purgatory (see p. 20)?

Pondering the Principles

1. Paul understood that our earthly bodies are decaying. Nevertheless, that awareness didn't cause him to neglect his body. He recognized that his body was the temple of God (1 Cor. 6:19). Judging from some of his metaphors (e.g., 1 Cor. 9:24-27), he was apparently an interested spectator of legitimate sports. Two extremes concerning how to treat our bodies are prevalent. Some believers neglect their bodies under the guise of spirituality and thereby fail to be good stewards of what God has given them. Others tend to spend much of their free time, energy, and money caring for their bodies, while practically ignoring any inner development. Are you guilty of either extreme? Determine today to be a good steward of the body God has given you, but concentrate on being the kind of person you ought to be.

2. Has your desire for heaven weakened? Is heaven and the presence of God less of a motivation for you than it used to be? Read 2 Corinthians 4:7–5:10. Then meditate on Paul's attitudes about heaven and what the passage reveals as the causes of those attitudes. Ask God to enable you to have a biblical perspective about heaven.

21

2
Looking Toward Heaven—Part 2
Where Heaven Is and What It Is Like

Outline

Introduction
A. The Inhabitants of Heaven
  1. God
  2. Holy angels
  3. Saints
B. The Supposed Intermediary State of Old Testament Saints
  1. The refutation
  2. The evidence
     a) In the psalms
        (1) Psalm 16
        (2) Psalm 23
     b) In Matthew 17
     c) In Luke 16
     d) In Luke 23

Review
 I. What Heaven Is

Lesson
 II. Where Heaven Is
   A. The Direction
   B. The Distance
III. What Heaven Is Like
   A. A General Overview
     1. By Ezekiel
     2. By John

a) Heaven's throne
   (1) Its Occupant
   (2) Its surroundings
   (3) Its observers
b) Heaven's Temple

Introduction

In Romans 12:12 Paul tells the Roman believers that they should be "rejoicing in hope." He was referring to the hope of heaven, which ought to fill us with joy. In contrast, the preacher of Ecclesiastes said, "The day of one's death is better than the day of one's birth" (7:1). Although he was being cynical because life was meaningless to him, as Christians we can agree with what he said because we have the hope of heaven. Paul said, "To me, to live is Christ, and to die is gain" (Phil. 1:21). The prospect of heaven made him joyful even in the face of death.

A. The Inhabitants of Heaven

1. God

   Heaven is the dwelling of God. Although God is present everywhere at all times, heaven is uniquely His home. Everything that is precious to us is in heaven: our Father, our Savior, our fellow believers, our name, our inheritance, our reward, our treasure, and our citizenship. Heaven is our home.

2. Holy angels

   Isaiah 6 pictures the Lord exalted on His heavenly throne, surrounded by holy angels (vv. 1-2). Matthew 22:30 and Luke 15:10 also state that the angels dwell in heaven.

3. Saints

   Heaven is where saints who have died now dwell and where believers who are alive will one day live. Although we are not in heaven, we live in the heavenlies —that is, we have a foretaste of heaven because the

24

Holy Spirit lives within us and works through us. In Christ, God has given us something of heaven's joy, love, power, and blessedness through the Spirit. The Holy Spirit is producing love, joy, peace, patience, kindness, goodness, faithfulness, gentleness, and self-control in every believer (Gal. 5:22-23), but those traits will not come to fruition until heaven. Therefore, the Spirit is the down payment of future blessings. Believers already enjoy heavenly blessings, but someday they will actually live there.

Both Old and New Testament believers who have died are in heaven, waiting until the second coming when they will receive their glorified bodies. All those who in faith accepted God's way of salvation—whether in Old or New Testament times—are now in the presence of God.

B. The Supposed Intermediary State of Old Testament Saints

1. The refutation

After many years of study, I believe that the moment any believer dies, he goes immediately to heaven. Some Medieval theologians taught that when an Old Testament saint died he entered what was later called *limbus patrum*—"the limbo of the fathers." According to that teaching, he entered a place where he had to wait until Christ died, when he could finally enter heaven. But the Bible nowhere verifies such an intermediary state. On the contrary, the evidence indicates that when a believer dies, he immediately enters the presence of God.

2. The evidence

a) In the psalms

(1) Psalm 16

In Psalm 16 the psalmist is hopeful even as he faces death: "Thou wilt not abandon my soul to Sheol; neither wilt Thou allow Thy Holy One to undergo decay. Thou wilt make known to me the path of life; in Thy presence is fullness of joy; in

Thy right hand there are pleasures forever" (vv. 10-11). The psalmist anticipated that when he left this world, he would enter the presence of God, finding pleasure and fullness of joy.

(2) Psalm 23

Psalm 23 says, "The Lord is my shepherd, I shall not want. He makes me lie down in green pastures; He leads me beside quiet waters. He restores my soul; He guides me in the paths of righteousness for His name's sake. Even though I walk through the valley of the shadow of death, I fear no evil; for Thou art with me; Thy rod and Thy staff, they comfort me. Thou dost prepare a table before me in the presence of my enemies; Thou hast anointed my head with oil; my cup overflows. Surely goodness and lovingkindness will follow me all the days of my life, and I will dwell in the house of the Lord forever." In the last verse the writer assumed that once his life was over, he would dwell in the house of the Lord, which can refer only to heaven. The hope of the psalmist was exactly the same as Paul's: "to be absent from the body and at home with the Lord" (2 Cor. 5:8).

b) In Matthew 17

When Christ was transfigured, Moses and Elijah appeared with Him (v. 3). Although Christ's death and resurrection hadn't yet occurred, Moses and Elijah were obviously safe in God's presence and were summoned to that wonderful occasion.

c) In Luke 16

We read that when the beggar Lazurus died, he "was carried away by the angels to Abraham's bosom" (v. 22). I believe that the place of blessedness where Abraham and Lazarus were seen was the presence of God. The Greek word translated "bosom" literally means "chest." The imagery is of an eastern banquet. Banquets were occasions for feasting, music, and conversation. They often lasted for days. The guests usually stayed at the host's home and frequently reclined at the table. They leaned on their elbows and reclined with their heads together, so that to someone across the table it appeared as if one person's head was resting on the other's chest. Apparently that was the positioning of John and Christ at the Last Supper (John 13:23). The guests positioned themselves that way so that they could converse while they ate with their free hands.

Being in Abraham's bosom meant reclining at a banquet table in a celebration of joy. In addition, Abraham is the most honored man in Jewish history. Being seated next to him meant you were seated next to the guest of honor. Lazurus, an ordinary beggar, was reclining at the table with the greatest man in Jewish history! The picture is of the house of God and the feast He prepares for those who come into His presence. Even though Lazurus had a diseased earthly life and had to beg to exist, he shared the place of honor with the greatest father of Israel.

d) In Luke 23

One of the thieves crucified with Christ said, " 'Jesus, remember me when You come in Your kingdom!' And [Jesus] said to him, 'Truly I say to you, today you shall be with Me in Paradise' " (vv. 42-43). Where is paradise? Some people say Christ is referring to an intermediary state. But another New Testament reference where the same word occurs clarifies its meaning. In 2 Corinthians 12:2-4 Paul discusses an experience he had that he didn't fully understand: "I know a man in Christ who fourteen years ago —whether in the body I do not know, or out of the body I do not know, God knows—such a man was caught up to the third heaven. And I know how such a man—whether in the body or apart from the body I do not know, God knows—was caught up into Paradise." It's reasonable to conclude that whatever paradise was before Christ's resurrection, it was the same thing at the time Paul wrote. Second Corinthians 12 makes it clear that paradise is a synonym for heaven.

When a saint died, he entered the presence of God—heaven itself—for the celebration and banquet that the Father had prepared. In heaven the saints know all the joy that God can possibly provide His children. Whether a believer died before or after Christ's resurrection, I believe he went home to be with the Lord.

Review

I. WHAT HEAVEN IS (see pp. 13-20)

Heaven is a place where God lives with His holy angels and the believers who have died. Heaven is also a sphere. Although many Christians still live in this world, they also live in the heavenlies. They enjoy a taste of heaven's benefits, such as eternal life and the fruit of the Spirit.

Lesson

II. WHERE HEAVEN IS

Heaven is an actual place. But it is impossible to chart the longitude or latitude of heaven, because it cannot be located geographically, even in space. But it's a place where people who have glorified bodies, like Christ's resurrection body, will actually live. After His resurrection Christ could eat, drink, walk, and talk. He could be touched and recognized when He allowed Himself to be. Heaven is a place for real, not ethereal, people.

A. The Direction

Heaven is located upward. In 2 Corinthians 12:2 Paul says that he was caught *up* to the third heaven. Ephesians 4:8-10 points out that when Jesus came to earth, He descended, and when He returned to heaven, He ascended. Acts 1 tells us that Jesus ascended into heaven. While the disciples watched, two angels said, "This Jesus, who has been taken up from you into heaven, will come in just the same way as you have watched Him go into heaven" (v. 11). Discussing the rapture, 1 Thessalonians 4:16-17 says the Lord will catch us up into heaven. When God examines His creatures, He looks down (Ps. 53:2); when man seeks God, he looks up (Ps. 121:1). The apostle John saw a door open in heaven and heard a voice inviting him to "come up" (Rev. 4:1). John pictured the New Jerusalem, the eternal home of the saints, as coming down out of heaven (Rev. 21:10).

B. The Distance

Second Corinthians 12:2 refers to the "third" heaven. From the earth's surface and extending upward 7-10 miles is a region called the troposphere; extending beyond that is the stratosphere; extending beyond that approximately 50 miles is the mesosphere; extending beyond that 250 miles or more is the ionosphere; extending beyond that to the outer limits of a planet's atmosphere is the exosphere, beyond which is infinite space. Beyond them all is the third heaven.

During 1973 and 1974 a Pioneer Spacecraft passed Jupiter, which is millions of miles from earth. Our most recent satellites are designed to go even farther. But none of them has reached heaven.

The moon is 252,000 miles from the earth, but that is still relatively close. If you walked twenty-four miles a day, theoretically you could arrive at the moon in approximately twenty-eight years, but you wouldn't be much closer to heaven.

A ray of light travels from the earth to the moon in about 1.5 seconds, because it is traveling 186,000 miles per second. Perhaps if we could travel at that incredible speed, we could reach heaven. Traveling 186,000 miles per second, we would arrive on the planet Mercury in about four minutes and thirty seconds because it is only 57 million miles from the earth. As we traveled to Mercury, we would reach Venus in about two minutes and twenty seconds because it is only 26 million miles away. To span the 390 million miles between Earth and Jupiter would take about thirty-five minutes. The 793 million miles to Saturn would take about an hour and ten minutes. Uranus, named for the Greek word *ouranos*, which means "heaven," is about 1.5 billion miles away. Neptune is about 2.7 billion miles away, and Pluto a billion more than that (Robert Jastrow and Malcolm Thompson, *Astronomy: Fundamentals and Frontiers* [Santa Barbara: John Wiley and Sons, 1977], p. 348). But after traveling that far, we would still be on the front porch of our solar system and well within our own galaxy!

The earth is one of nine planets revolving around the sun. Earth has a diameter of 8,000 miles and an estimated mass of about 6.6×10^{21} tons. That massive sphere revolves on its axis, remaining 93 million miles from our sun. The sun has a diameter of about 864 thousand miles and a mass 332 thousand times larger than the earth. But it's only one star in a galaxy of billions of other stars! Distances in the universe are so great that they have to be measured by the speed of light, which is 186,000 miles per second or 11,160,000 miles per minute. For example, our sun is about eight light minutes away.

Our solar system has a diameter of approximately 700 light minutes—8 billion miles—but the galaxy that contains it has a diameter of 100,000 light years and is one of billions of galaxies (*Astronomy: Fundamentals and Frontiers*, pp. 4, 12). Nevertheless, Jesus said to the thief dying next to Him, "*Today* you shall be with Me in Paradise" (Luke 23:43, emphasis added). Only God could bridge such distances.

III. WHAT HEAVEN IS LIKE

A. A General Overview

1. By Ezekiel

Our first view of heaven comes from the prophet Ezekiel. God wonderfully revealed to him by a vision what heaven is like. Ezekiel 1:4-28 says, "As I looked, behold, a storm wind was coming from the north, a great cloud with fire flashing forth continually and a bright light around it, and in its midst something like glowing metal in the midst of the fire. And within it there were figures resembling four living beings. And this was their appearance: they had human form. Each of them had four faces and four wings. And their legs were straight and their feet were like a calf's hoof, and they gleamed like burnished bronze. Under their wings on their four sides were human hands. As for the faces and wings of the four of them, their wings touched one another; their faces did not turn when they moved, each went straight forward. As for the form of their faces, each had the face of a man, all four had the face of a lion on the right and the face of a bull on the left, and all four had the face of an eagle. Such were their faces. Their wings were spread out above; each had two touching another being, and two covering their bodies. And each went straight forward; wherever the spirit was about to go, they would go, without turning as they went. In the midst of the living beings there was something that looked like burning coals of fire, like torches darting back and forth among the living beings. The fire was bright, and lightning was flashing from the fire. And the living beings ran to and fro like bolts of lightning.

"Now as I looked at the living beings, behold, there was one wheel on the earth beside the living beings, for each of the four of them. The appearance of the wheels and their workmanship was like sparkling beryl [a multicolored stone], and all four of them had the same form, their appearance and workmanship being as if one wheel were within another. Whenever they moved, they moved in any of their four directions, without turning as they moved. As for their rims they were lofty and awesome, and the rims of all four of them were full of eyes round about. And whenever the living beings moved, the wheels moved with them. And whenever the living beings rose from the earth, the wheels rose also. Wherever the spirit was about to go, they would go in that direction. And the wheels rose close beside them; for the spirit of the living beings was in the wheels. Whenever those went, these went; and whenever those stood still, these stood still. And whenever those rose from the earth, the wheels rose close beside them; for the spirit of the living beings was in the wheels.

"Now over the heads of the living beings there was something like an expanse, like the awesome gleam of crystal, extended over their heads. And under the expanse their wings were stretched out straight, one to-

31

ward the other; each one also had two wings covering their bodies on the one side and on the other. I also heard the sound of their wings like the sound of abundant waters as they went, like the voice of the Almighty, a sound of tumult like the sound of an army camp; whenever they stood still, they dropped their wings. And there came a voice from above the expanse that was over their heads; whenever they stood still, they dropped their wings.

"Now above the expanse that was over their heads there was something resembling a throne, like lapis lazuli in appearance; and on that which resembled a throne, high up, was a figure with the appearance of a man. Then I noticed from the appearance of His loins and upward something like glowing metal that looked like fire all around within it, and from the appearance of His lions and downward I saw something like fire; and there was a radiance around Him. As the appearance of the rainbow in the clouds on a rainy day, so was the appearance of the surrounding radiance. Such was the appearance of the likeness of the glory of the Lord. And when I saw it, I fell on my face."

That was Ezekiel's description of God's throne in heaven. We cannot fully understand all he described, and neither did he. But under the inspiration of the Holy Spirit he attempted to describe what he saw: blazing light reflected off polished jewels and colored wheels of light mingled with angelic beings (the "living beings"). Around the throne of the eternal, glorious God, he saw a flashing, sparkling, spinning rainbow of brilliance. In referring to the faces of the angelic creatures some say the lion refers to majesty and power, the man to intelligence and will, the ox to patient service, and the eagle to swift judgment. Although it is difficult to interpret the specifics, we can say this is describing the sovereignty, majesty, and glory of God and the incredible beauty, symmetry, and perfection of His heaven. The wheels that moved in concert, the flashing lightning, the sparkling jewels, and the brilliant light all picture God's glory. Ezekiel gave us a picture of heaven, but it's beyond our ability to fathom.

2. By John

In the book of Revelation we begin to see more of the details. The Greek word translated "heaven" occurs more than fifty times in the book. Twice God is called "the God of heaven" (11:13; 16:11). In chapter 4 John says, "After these things I looked, and behold, a door standing open in heaven, and the first voice which I had heard, like the sound of a trumpet speaking with me, said, 'Come up here, and I will show you what must take place after these things.' Immediately I was in the Spirit; and behold, a throne was standing in heaven, and One sitting on the throne" (vv. 1-2).

a) Heaven's throne

Ezekiel ended chapter 1 with a description of God's throne and the inexplicable glory of heaven. John begins by describing that throne. Repeatedly in this passage he mentions the throne, which is the center of heaven and the focal point of God's presence.

(1) Its Occupant

Verse 3 says, "He who was sitting was like a jasper stone." Jasper is an opaque crystalline quartz of differing colors, especially shades of green. The jasper of ancient times was more transparent. Verse 3 adds that God was like "a sardius in appearance." The red sardius may speak of God as Redeemer, the One who provided a blood sacrifice. If that is its significance, it highlights the glory of God's redemptive character. Jasper and Sardius were the first and last of the twelve stones on the breastplate of the high priest (Ex. 28:17, 20). They represented Reuben, Jacob's oldest son, and Benjamin, his youngest. Thus in a sense God pictures Himself as embracing Israel.

(2) Its surroundings

Sounding much like Ezekiel, John continues, "There was a rainbow around the throne, like an emerald in appearance. . . . And from the throne proceed flashes of lightning and sounds and peals of thunder" (vv. 3-5). At Mount Sinai, when God came down to give the law, thunder and lightning accompanied Him (Ex. 19:16). The writers of Scripture, seeking to describe the indescribable, portray the presence of God as filled with thunder and lightning, blinding light, and a sparkling, dazzling array of colors and rainbows. John continues his description of the scene around the throne: "There were seven lamps of fire burning before the throne, which are the seven Spirits of God" (v. 5). That does not teach that there are seven Holy Spirits. Rather there is one sevenfold Spirit, described in Isaiah 11:2 as (1) the Spirit of the Lord, (2) the spirit of wisdom, (3) the spirit of understanding, (4) the spirit of counsel, (5) the spirit of strength, (6) the spirit of knowledge, and (7) the spirit of the fear of the Lord.

Verse 6 says, "Before the throne there was, as it were, a sea of glass like crystal." Picture the beauty of that scene: a brilliant rainbow and the flashing colors of emerald, sardius, and jasper all splashing off a sea of crystal! Scripture uses color, light, and crystal to reflect the splendor and majesty of the throne of God. In Exodus 24 "Moses went up with Aaron, Nadab and Abihu, and seventy of the elders of Israel, and they saw the God of Israel; and under His feet there appeared to be a pavement of sapphire, as clear as the sky itself" (vv. 9-10).

That is a description of heaven. Heaven is the actual place where God dwells. In heaven is a throne from which comes flashing and sparkling light, and beneath it is a crystal clear, brilliant, sparkling sea of glass. It is described as sapphire in one passage because of the color reflecting off it and as clear in another because it picks up the color that sparkles from the presence of the One who occupies the throne. Ezekiel described it as the color of dazzling crystal stretched across the sky.

Glimpses of Heaven?

Heaven is not a land of shadows and mists. Some people who were supposedly dead and then resuscitated claim to have seen heaven. When asked what heaven was like, many have said it was like a light at the end of a long tunnel. Books describing such experiences are popular. But heaven is not some light at end of a dark tunnel; its brilliance is magnificent beyond description!

(3) Its observers

In Revelation 4:4 John says, "Around the throne were twenty-four thrones; and upon the thrones I saw twenty-four elders sitting, clothed in white garments and golden crowns on their heads." I believe those elders represent the new priesthood, the church in heaven. We will be reigning with God in the midst of a crystal sea that flashes and sparkles with His splendor. Verse 6 adds that around the throne were four living creatures— probably a reference to angelic beings, perhaps cherubim. Surrounding the throne is the angelic host and the redeemed church; occupying the throne is God Himself in all the glory of His majestic revelation.

b) Heaven's Temple

The two major buildings of any ancient city were the palace and the temple. They represented human and divine rule. In heaven there is a throne, which portrays God as the majestic Sovereign, and a Temple, which portrays Him as One who should be worshiped. In Revelation 3:12 Christ says, "He who overcomes [referring to the Christian], I will make him a pillar in the temple of My God, and he will not go out from it anymore." Believers will be the pillars of God's Temple. In Revelation 7:15 one of the twenty-four elders, speaking of saints who have come out of the Great Tribulation, says, "They are before the throne of God; and they serve Him day and night in His temple; and He who sits on the throne shall spread His tabernacle over them." Christians will

35

serve God in that Temple. In Revelation 11:19 John says, "The temple of God which is in heaven was opened; and the ark of His covenant appeared in His temple, and there were flashes of lightning and sounds and peals of thunder and an earthquake and a great hailstorm." In chapter 15 John says, "I looked, and the temple of the tabernacle of testimony in heaven was opened" (v. 5). Those passages make clear that there is a Temple in heaven.

In Revelation 21:22, however, John says, "I saw no temple in it [the New Jerusalem], for the Lord God, the Almighty, and the Lamb, are its temple." The Temple of that city isn't a place where God dwells— God Himself is the Temple. Attempting to reconcile Revelation 21:22 with the previous passages, some Bible scholars argue that though at present there is a Temple in heaven, when God constructs the new heavens and earth, there won't be. However, I believe that Revelation 21:22 defines the Temple—it isn't a building; it's the Lord Himself. By saying that believers will be pillars in that Temple, Christ promised us a place forever in the presence of God.

Focusing on the Facts

1. Who are the inhabitants of heaven (see p. 24)?
2. Explain the teaching of *limbus patrum* (see p. 25).
3. What passages in the psalms imply that there was no intermediary state for Old Testament believers? Explain (see pp. 25-26).
4. Explain the phrase "Abraham's bosom" (Luke 16:22; see pp. 26-27).
5. Where is "paradise"? Support your answer with Scripture (see p. 27).
6. According to the Bible, heaven is in what direction (see p. 28)?
7. What Old Testament prophet gives us the first comprehensive view of heaven? In what chapter of his book (see p. 30)?
8. Summarize that prophet's description of heaven (see pp. 30-32).
9. What may be the significance of the sardius stone in Revelation 4:3 (see p. 33)?

10. In what Old Testament context were the jasper and sardius stones used together? What is the significance of the stones in Revelation 4:3 (Ex. 28:17, 20; see p. 33)?
11. What does John mean by "the seven Spirits of God" (Isa. 11:2; see p. 34)?
12. Why is the sea before God's throne likened to sapphire in one passage and clear glass in another (see p. 34)?
13. Whom does John see around the throne (see p. 35)?
14. Explain Revelation 21:22. How can one reconcile its meaning with passages such as Revelation 11:19 (see p. 36)?

Pondering the Principles

1. As believers, we have the hope that once we leave these bodies, we will enter the presence of God. Christ's death and resurrection assure us of that hope, freeing us from the fear of death (Heb. 2:14-15). Knowing that death ushers us into God's presence is a great comfort because each of us will have to face death (Phil. 1:21-24). God also uses such knowledge to comfort us when we have to deal with the death of a family member or close friend (1 Thess. 4:13-14). First Corinthians 15 tells us that ultimately we will see death completely destroyed and will receive imperishable bodies. Take time now to meditate on those truths and thank God for the sacrifice of Christ by which He delivered "those who through fear of death were subject to slavery all their lives" (Heb. 2:15).

2. Seeing Ezekiel and the apostle John struggle to describe the indescribable, we understand that even if God had revealed all the details about heaven, we wouldn't be able to know or understand them. It's so unlike what we know. But in Ephesians 2 Paul gives us an insight into heaven that we can understand because it draws on our experience. Read verses 1-6, noting the incredible grace that God demonstrated in saving you. Aren't you overwhelmed each day with God's grace to you? Now read Ephesians 2:7. Although no description exists of what heaven looks like, note the vivid description of what it will be like: "In the ages to come [God will] show the surpassing riches of His grace in kindness toward us in Christ Jesus." Since you have experienced the riches of His grace in your life here, you can look with anticipation toward the greater riches of heaven.

3
Looking Toward Heaven—Part 3
The New Jerusalem

Outline

Review
I. What Heaven Is
II. Where Heaven Is
III. What Heaven Is Like
   A. A General Overview
      1. By Ezekiel
      2. By John
         a) Heaven's throne
         b) Heaven's Temple

Lesson
   B. A Specific Focus
      1. The new heaven and earth
         a) Prophesied
         b) Created
         c) Illustrated
         d) Described
      2. The New Jerusalem
         a) Its preparation
         b) Its identification
            (1) The capital of heaven
            (2) The dwelling of Christ's Bride
         c) Its description

(1) The glory of the city
(2) The design of the city
   (*a*) Its walls
   (*b*) Its measurements
   (*c*) Its materials
(3) The distinctions of the city

Conclusion

Review

I. WHAT HEAVEN IS (see pp. 13-20)

II. WHERE HEAVEN IS (see pp. 28-30)

III. WHAT HEAVEN IS LIKE

A. A General Overview (see pp. 30-36)

1. By Ezekiel (see pp. 30-32)

2. By John (see pp. 33-36)

a) Heaven's throne (see pp. 33-35)

The book of Revelation mentions the throne of God thirty-nine times. God's throne is the focal point of heaven—and from it emanates flashing, brilliant light.

b) Heaven's Temple (see pp. 35-36)

Revelation 3:12 says that there is a Temple in heaven, which the saints never leave. The Temple is immense, infinite, and eternal. In fact, the Lord Himself and the Lamb are the Temple (Rev. 21:22). In the eternal heaven God will spread His infinite presence over His people as a Temple.

B. A Specific Focus

1. The new heaven and earth

Revelation 21 describes in more detail what heaven is like by describing the new heaven and earth. In the universe the stellar bodies, moons, and planets compose the present heaven, and we occupy the earth. One day God will renovate the universe and make a new heaven and earth.

a) Prophesied

The Old Testament prophets spoke of that renovation. Through the prophet Isaiah, God said, "Behold, I create new heavens and a new earth; and the former things shall not be remembered or come to mind. But be glad and rejoice forever in what I create" (65:17-18). In Isaiah 66:22 God says, "The new heavens and the new earth which I make will endure before Me." Quoting Psalm 102:25-27, Hebrews 1:10-12 says, "Thou, Lord, in the beginning didst lay the foundation of the earth, and the heavens are the works of Thy hands; they will perish, but Thou remainest; and they all will become old as a garment, and as a mantle Thou wilt roll them up; as a garment they will also be changed. But Thou art the same, and Thy years will not come to an end." One day God will change the present heaven and earth.

b) Created

By the time we reach Revelation 21, the Battle of Armageddon has been fought, the thousand-year, earthly reign of Christ has come to an end, and at the great white throne God has sentenced Satan and all the ungodly to eternal hell. Then the whole universe, except hell, is dissolved, and God reveals a new heaven and new earth so magnificent that no one remembers the first. In 2 Peter 3:13 Peter describes it: "According to His promise [Psalm 102; Isaiah 65-66] we are looking for new heavens and a new earth, in which righteousness dwells." Since Satan fell, the earth and the first two heavens have been under God's curse. In Genesis 3:17 God says, "Cursed is the ground because of you." Job 15:15 says, "The heavens are not pure in His sight." Isaiah 24:5 says, "The earth is also polluted by its inhabitants." We live in a polluted universe, but God is going to remake it.

c) Illustrated

Peter said that we are to know "this first of all, that in the last days mockers will come with their mocking, following after their own lusts, and saying, 'Where is the promise of His coming? For ever since the fathers fell asleep, all continues just as it was from the beginning of creation' " (2 Peter 3:3-4). The men Peter describes reason that since there never has been a cataclysmic judgment on the earth, there never will be—which is as logical as saying, "I know I'll never die because I haven't yet."

Verses 5-6 continue, "When they maintain this, it escapes their notice that by the word of God the heavens existed long ago and the earth was formed out of water and by water, through which the world at that time was destroyed, being flooded with water." Those who say there has been no cataclysmic judgment on the earth forget (perhaps purposefully) about the Flood, when God drowned the entire human race, sparing only Noah and his family. Prior to the Flood, a canopy of water encircled the earth, protecting it from the sun's ultraviolet rays. Because of that protection, plant life flourished, and men and animals lived hundreds of years. But because of man's sin, God caused the canopy to inundate the earth. Peter is saying that the Flood illustrates the day when God will renovate the entire earth again but in a much greater way than the Genesis Flood— He will destroy the whole earth.

Verses 6-7 say, "The world at that time was destroyed, being flooded with water. But the present heavens and earth by His word are being reserved for fire, kept for the day of judgment and destruction of ungodly men." Verse 10 says, "The day of the Lord will come like a thief, in which the heavens will pass away with a roar and the elements will be destroyed with intense heat, and the earth and its works will be burned up." Atomic science has demonstrated that such destruction can occur. By splitting the atom, man unleashed the potential for unbelievable destruction—a chain reaction of atomic explosions could literally disintegrate this earth.

Our earth has tremendous potential for fire. We live on the crust of a fireball; most of the earth's approximately eight thousand mile diameter is molten flame. The earth's core is a flaming, boiling, liquid lake of fire, which sometimes bursts through the earth's crust as a volcano. One day God will unleash His power and destroy the whole universe with fire.

d) Described

Revelation 21:1 speaks of "a new heaven and a new earth." The Greek word translated "new" (*kainos*) stresses that the earth God will create will not merely be new as opposed to old, but will also be different in character. Paul uses the same Greek word in 2 Corinthians 5:17: "If any man is in Christ, he is a new creature." The quality has changed. The new heavens and earth, like our newness in Christ, will be glorified, free from sin's curse, and eternal.

I cannot tell you what the new heaven will look like, but I do know that there will be no more tempests, thunderbolts, or demons. Today our earth has spots of beauty carpeted with grass, flowers, crops, and shady trees, spanned by snow-capped mountains, and flowing with crystal streams. Nevertheless, the earth is marred by disease, death, pollution, and the miseries of godlessness. But our present heavens "will be destroyed by burning, and the elements will melt with intense heat" (2 Peter 3:12). Then God will create "new heavens and a new earth, in which righteousness dwells" (v. 13). Only then will the universe stop groaning under the curse of sin (cf. Rom. 8:19-22). Every believer will live in that new earth. Matthew 5:5 says, "Blessed are the gentle, for they shall inherit the earth." When that day comes it will be unnecessary to pray for God's will to be done on earth as it is in heaven, for God will indeed be reigning on earth.

In Revelation 21:1 John adds, "There is no longer any sea." That intriguing statement can be interpreted several different ways. Some Bible scholars interpret it to mean that no national boundaries will exist. Others point out that the sea symbolized fear to the ancients, and thus an absence of sea implied the absence of fear. Both are correct. In the new heaven and earth nothing will make us afraid, and nothing will separate us from other people. In Revelation 22:1-2 John says that the only water in heaven is the "river of the water of life, clear as crystal, coming from the throne of God and of the Lamb, in the middle of its street. And on either side of the river [is] the tree of life." Coming out of God's throne and flowing down heaven's main street is a crystal-clear river. There will be no more boundaries, separation, or mysterious, violent seas.

2. The New Jerusalem

   a) Its preparation

   In Revelation 21:2 John says, "I saw the holy city, new Jerusalem, coming down out of heaven from God, made ready as a bride adorned for her husband." The phrase "made ready" implies that the new Jerusalem has already been completed. John doesn't say that he saw it being created but instead says that he saw it "coming down out of heaven from God." Since God dwells in the third heaven, we can conclude that He has prepared this city to eventually become the capital city of the final state. Apparently

44

when the new heaven and earth are finished, the new Jerusalem will come down out of the third heaven, where it will have already been completed. When Christ told His disciples that He was going away to "prepare a place" for them (John 14:3), He may have been referring to the new Jerusalem.

b) Its identification

(1) The capital of heaven

Three Jerusalems are mentioned in the Bible: the historical Jerusalem, the millennial Jerusalem, and the eternal Jerusalem (which I believe will be the capital city of eternity). The eternal Jerusalem is not heaven; it is the capital city of heaven. Its "architect and builder is God" (Heb. 11:10). The writer of Hebrews said, "You have come to Mount Zion and to the city of the living God, the heavenly Jerusalem, and to myriads of angels, to the general assembly and church of the first-born who are enrolled in heaven, and to God, the Judge of all, and to the spirits of righteous men made perfect, and to Jesus" (12:22-24).

(2) The dwelling of Christ's Bride

The New Jerusalem is described "as a bride adorned for her husband" (Rev. 21:2). One of the greatest ways to express beauty is to liken something to the beauty of a bride. Such a designation reminds us that the church, Christ's Bride, will dwell there. Revelation 19:9 tells us that when the saints convene in the Lord's presence, they will attend a marriage supper. In Revelation 21:9-10 an angel says to John, "Come here, I shall show you the bride, the wife of the Lamb. And he carried me away in the Spirit to a great and high mountain, and showed me the holy city, Jerusalem, coming down out of heaven from God."

Although the New Jerusalem is uniquely identified as the bride's city because of the church, I believe the saints of all the ages will be there: Old

45

Testament saints, the church, and Tribulation saints. But if that is true, why did John uniquely identify it as the bride's city? The book of Revelation was written to comfort the persecuted church. Persecuted Christians in the first century read about a city that belonged to them and were given comfort and hope.

c) Its description

In Revelation 21:9-10 we saw that an angel took John in a vision to a mountain on the new earth from which he could watch God's masterpiece, the capital city of the infinite heaven, descend from God out of heaven.

(1) The glory of the city

John described the city as having the "glory of God" (v. 11). The essence of the eternal heaven is that God's glory is manifest in it. Isaiah 60:19 says, "No longer will you have the sun for light by day, nor for brightness will the moon give you light; but you will have the Lord for an everlasting light, and your God for your glory." Revelation 21:23 says, "The city has no need of the sun or of the moon to shine upon it, for the glory of God has illumined it, and its lamp is the Lamb." God Himself will light all of the infinite heaven, particularly the sparkling celestial jewel called the New Jerusalem.

In verse 11 John tries to describe it: "Her brilliance was like a very costly stone, as a stone of crystal-clear jasper." When I was growing up, I used to go roller skating. Hanging in the middle of the rink was a sphere covered with small, mirrored squares. When lights were aimed at it, the whole rink flashed and sparkled with light. In a mundane way that is similar to the picture John was trying to communicate: he saw the eternal city coming down from heaven, resembling a sparkling, crystal, diamond-like stone blazing with the glory of God's very nature. And the

46

splashing light of God's glory literally covered the infinite universe with breathtaking beauty.

(2) The design of the city

In Revelation 21:12—22:5 John attempts to describe the indescribable.

(a) Its walls

Verse 12 says, "It had a great and high wall." The wall probably symbolizes security and protection. In ancient times people expected cities to be safe and secure. Revelation 22:14-15 says, "Blessed are those who wash their robes, that they may have the right to the tree of life, and may enter by the gates into the city. Outside are the dogs and the sorcerers and the immoral persons and the murderers and the idolaters, and everyone who loves and practices lying." Therefore, the walls and gates testify that some can enter and others cannot. The wall is "seventy-two yards, according to human measurements, which are also angelic measurements" (Rev. 21:17).

Along the wall were "twelve gates, and at the gates twelve angels; and names are written on them, which are . . . the twelve tribes of the sons of Israel" (v. 12). Since the gates of the bride's city are named after the tribes of Israel, exhibiting God's eternal covenant relationship with Israel, that leads us to conclude that Old Testament saints will live there. Apparently twelve is the number of perfect symmetry: twelve gates, twelve angels, and twelve tribes (v. 12), twelve foundations, twelve apostles (v. 14), twelve pearls (v. 21), and twelve kinds of fruit (22:2). John records that there were "three gates on the east and three gates on the north and three gates on the south and three gates on the west" (21:13). Gates imply that people leave and enter the city. Do not think that the city contains us for-

47

ever; we have the infinite universe to travel, and when we do, we will go in and out through those gates.

Verse 14 says, "The wall of the city had twelve foundation stones, and on them were the twelve names of the twelve apostles of the Lamb." God is identifying Himself with His new covenant people. Notice that Jesus Christ is referred to as "the Lamb"—He will forever be known by His sacrificial name.

(b) Its measurements

In verses 15-16 John says, "The one who spoke with me had a gold measuring rod [probably about ten feet long] to measure the city, and its gates and its wall. And the city is laid out as a square, and its length is as great as the width; and he measured the city with the rod, fifteen hundred miles; its length and width and height are equal." John describes the city as a perfectly symmetrical, fifteen-hundred mile cube. In Solomon's Temple the Holy of Holies was a cube of twenty cubits (1 Kings 6:20). The New Jerusalem is the Holy of Holies for eternity.

According to Revelation 21:16 the New Jerusalem is 1,500 miles long, wide, and high. That means it contains 2.25 million square miles, amazing when you consider that Greater London is 621 square miles. The city of London is one square mile and has a population of about 5,000. On that basis, the New Jerusalem would be able to house more than 100 billion people! The New Jerusalem is large enough for the few who find the narrow way (Matt. 7:13-14), but it won't confine them. This cube, having about the same dimensions as the distance from Maine to Florida, apparently has multiple levels and millions of intersecting golden avenues. It is a place of incredible majesty and beauty.

(c) Its materials

Revelation 21:18 says, "The material of the wall was jasper [a transparent, diamondlike stone]." The transparent stone will allow the glory of God radiating from the center of the city to shine through. Verse 18 continues, "The city was pure gold, like clear glass." The gold we are familiar with is certainly not clear. What John saw must have sparkled with a brilliance and glow that had a golden tone but was still crystal clear. In addition, in our glorified bodies our perceptions will be different—something might appear to us as being both solid and transparent.

Both Ezekiel and John describe much of heaven as being transparent. The radiance of God's glory reflects the beauty of His presence through every diamond facet. Verse 19 says, "The foundation stones of the city wall were adorned with every kind of precious stone. The first foundation stone was jasper; the second, sapphire; the third, chalcedony; the fourth, emerald; the fifth, sardonyx; the sixth, sardius; the seventh, chrysolite; the eighth, beryl; the ninth, topaz; the tenth, chrysoprase; the eleventh, jacinth; the twelfth, amethyst." Those colored jewels, along with the transparent glass, diamonds, and golden hue, form a picture of unbelievable and indescribable beauty. God has planted within us a love of beauty—and heaven's surpassing beauty will satisfy that love forever.

Verse 21 adds, "The twelve gates were twelve pearls; each one of the gates was a single pearl. And the street of the city was pure gold, like transparent glass." John doesn't tell us how big the gates are, but he does say that each gate is a single pearl.

(3) The distinctions of the city

(*a*) Its Temple

John said, "I saw no temple in it, for the Lord
God, the Almighty, and the Lamb, are its
temple" (v. 22). Heaven's Temple is the presence of God.

(*b*) Its light

Verse 23 says, "The city has no need of the
sun or of the moon to shine upon it, for the
glory of God has illumined it, and its lamp is
the Lamb." The presence of God and the
Lamb will light the entire city. In fact, Isaiah
said, "The moon will be abashed and the sun
ashamed" (24:23). Revelation 21:24 adds that
"the nations shall walk by its light, and the
kings of the earth shall bring their glory into
it." John is saying that even the kings of the
earth will give up their glory for the glory of
heaven. All nations will walk in the light of
God's presence, and all men, regardless of
their position, will bow to His glory.

(*c*) Its security

Verse 25 says, "In the daytime (for there shall
be no night there) its gates shall never be
closed." In an ancient city the gates were shut
at night to protect the people from robbers,
bandits, and invading armies. Gates that are
always open speak of perfect security and
protection. Verse 26 says, "They shall bring
the glory and honor of the nations into it."
Nothing will rival God's glory.

(*d*) Its citizens

In verse 27 John says, "Nothing unclean and
no one who practices abomination and lying,
shall ever come into it, but only those whose
names are written in the Lamb's book of life"

50

(cf. Rev. 22:15). Only those who put their trust in Christ will enter that great city.

(e) Its refreshments

In Revelation 22:1-2 the angel shows John "a river of the water of life, clear as crystal, coming from the throne of God and of the Lamb, in the middle of its street. And on either side of the river was the tree of life, bearing twelve kinds of fruit, yielding its fruit every month; and the leaves of the tree were for the healing of the nations." In Eden a beautiful river watered the garden; in the New Jerusalem a crystal-clear, celestial river flows out of the throne and through the middle of the city. Psalm 46:4 says, "There is a river whose streams make glad the city of God."

Imagine what a river meant to someone living in a barren place like Palestine. A river was a welcome place of comfort and rest, refreshment and sustenance. It meant cool water to a mouth parched by the desert heat. The New Jerusalem will be the epitome of everything precious—a city, a river, and trees. Imagine the joy of someone who lived in the desert finding a tree with fruit!

In heaven we will eat for enjoyment, not sustenance. The Greek word translated "healing" is *therapeia*, from which we get the English word *therapeutic*. John is saying that the leaves of the tree of life promote the enrichment of life—they are for the pure joy of eating. The water of life is for the sheer joy of drinking. Food won't be needed in heaven, but it will be enjoyed.

(f) Its fellowship

The apostle John continues, "There shall no longer be any curse; and the throne of God and of the Lamb shall be in it, and His bond-

51

servants shall serve Him; and they shall see His face, and His name shall be on their foreheads. And there shall no longer be any night; and they shall not have need of the light of a lamp nor the light of the sun, because the Lord God shall illumine them; and they shall reign forever and ever" (vv. 3-5). First Thessalonians 4:17 says that after the rapture "we shall always be with the Lord." Seeing His face (v. 4) implies intimacy, communion, and fellowship. Having His name on our forehead speaks of His ownership.

John is saying that sinners will fellowship intimately in the presence of a holy God forever. Christians speak of being with the eternal God, of having intimate fellowship with Christ, of being joint heirs with Christ. They assert that they will judge the world and rule with Christ. All those statements would be blasphemous if God had not promised them to us.

Conclusion

Years ago Lutheran commentator J. A. Seiss wrote these beautiful words about the heavenly Jerusalem: "That shining is not from any material combustion,—not from any consumption of fuel that needs to be replaced as one supply burns out; for it is the uncreated light of Him who is light, dispensed by and through the Lamb as the everlasting lamp, to the home, and hearts, and understandings, of His glorified saints. When Paul and Silas lay wounded and bound in the inner dungeon of the prison of Philippi, they still had sacred light which enabled them to beguile the night-watches with happy songs. When Paul was on his way to Damascus, a light brighter than the sun at noon shone round about him, irradiating his whole being with new sights and understanding, and making his soul and body ever afterward light in the Lord. When Moses came down from the mount of his communion with God, his face was so luminous that his brethren could not endure to look upon it. He was in such close fellowship with light that he became informed with light, and came to the camp as a very lamp of God, glowing with the glory of God.

"On the Mount of Transfiguration, that same light streamed forth from all the body and raiment of the blessed Jesus. And with reference to the very time when this city comes into being and place, Isaiah says, 'The moon shall be ashamed and the sun confounded,'—ashamed because of the out-beaming glory which then shall appear in the New Jerusalem, leaving no more need for them to shine in it, since the glory of God lights it, and the Lamb is the light thereof" (*The Apocalypse: Lectures on the Book of Revelation* [Grand Rapids: Zondervan, 1970 reprint], p. 499). Paul said, "Things which eye has not seen and ear has not heard, and which have not entered the heart of man, all that God has prepared for those who love Him" (1 Cor. 2:9).

Focusing on the Facts

1. Was the apostle John the first to mention the new heaven and earth? Explain (see p. 41).
2. When will the creation of the new heaven and earth take place (see p. 41)?
3. What answer does Peter give to those who deny a future cataclysmic judgment by arguing that one has never occurred (2 Peter 3:5-6; see p. 42)?
4. Explain why men and animals lived so much longer before the Flood than they do now (see p. 42).
5. What does "no more sea" probably imply (see p. 44)?
6. According to Revelation 21:2, when is the New Jerusalem constructed (see pp. 44-45)?
7. How is the New Jerusalem identified (see p. 45)?
8. The wall probably symbolizes _____ and _____ (see p. 47).
9. What is the significance of God's naming the gates of the bride's city after the tribes of Israel (see p. 47)?
10. Describe the dimensions of the city (see p. 48).
11. How will the city be lighted (see p. 50)?
12. What do all the citizens of the New Jerusalem have in common (see pp. 50-51)?
13. Describe the refreshments of the city (see p. 51).
14. What does the phrase "they shall see His face" imply (Rev. 22:4; see p. 52)?

Pondering the Principles

1. In 2 Peter 3 Peter graphically describes the certain destruction of the present heavens and earth. It's ironic that what many people focus on will be destroyed. In fact, the apostle John uses that coming destruction as part of his argument against loving the world. Read 1 John 2:15-17, noting in verse 16 the three attitudes that are part of the world (Gk., *kosmos*, "world-system"). Do any of those attitudes characterize your life or values? Are you becoming attached to what will eventually be burned? If the world has influenced your values and attitudes, obey John's directive: Stop loving the world, because it "is passing away, and also its lusts; but the one who does the will of God abides forever" (v. 17). Ask God to change your values and attitudes and to conform them to His Word.

2. Revelation 22:4 points to the fellowship and communion we will enjoy with God in eternity. Unfortunately, many Christians believe that such fellowship is impossible until then. But passages such as 1 John 5:11-12 clearly demonstrate that eternal life isn't something that we receive after we enter heaven but is ours to enjoy right now. And in John 17:3 Christ mentions this vital aspect of eternal life: "This is eternal life, that they may know Thee, the only true God, and Jesus Christ whom Thou hast sent." As Christians we can commune and fellowship with God even now through prayer and the study of His Word. Have you neglected the wonderful privilege of communing with the eternal God? Take time now to rearrange your priorities so that you can emphasize your relationship with God and not life's trivia.

4
Looking Toward Heaven—Part 4
What We Will Be Like

Outline

Introduction
A. The New Person
B. The Constant Problem

Review
I. What Heaven Is
II. Where Heaven Is
III. What Heaven Is Like

Lesson
IV. What We Will Be Like
A. A Perfected Soul
1. Required
2. Described
a) Negatively
b) Positively
(1) Perfect pleasure
(2) Perfect knowledge
(3) Perfect comfort
(4) Perfect love
(5) Perfect joy
B. A Perfected Body
1. The promise of resurrection
2. The body of resurrection
a) Its distinctiveness
(1) Illustrated by the death of a seed
(2) Illustrated by the differing animal bodies
(3) Illustrated by the differing celestial bodies

b) Its characteristics
  (1) Imperishable
  (2) Glorious
  (3) Powerful
  (4) Spiritual
  (5) Christlike

Conclusion

Introduction

The Bible teaches that believers will experience eternal perfection of the whole person—body and soul. Heaven is a perfect place for people made perfect. The purpose of salvation is to make us perfect, so that we can dwell in God's presence forever. The ultimate expression of salvation is perfection. The new birth begins the process by transforming the inner person.

A. The New Person

When someone puts his faith in Jesus Christ, he becomes "a new creature" (2 Cor. 5:17). Colossians 2:10 says that he is "made complete" in Christ. Peter adds in 2 Peter 1:3 that believers have "everything pertaining to life and godliness." If you are a Christian, the life of God dwells in your soul. You are a new person. In Romans 6:18 Paul says we "became slaves of righteousness." We have new life. Instead of being slaves of sin, we are servants of righteousness. Instead of receiving the wages of sin, which is death, we have received God's gift of eternal life (Rom. 6:23).

B. The Constant Problem

A problem exists, however: our new inner nature is incarcerated in human flesh. In Romans 7 Paul says, "That which I am doing, I do not understand; for I am not practicing what I would like to do, but I am doing the very thing I hate. But if I do the very thing I do not wish to do, I agree with the Law, confessing that it is good. So now, no longer am I the one doing it, but sin which indwells me" (vv. 15-

17). Paul was establishing an important principle: although the believer is a new creation and has a new life principle, that new life isn't able to fully express itself because of the presence of sin.

In verse 18 Paul says, "I know that nothing good dwells in me, that is, in my flesh." By "flesh" Paul meant not merely his physical body but the totality of human fallenness. His mind, emotions, and will still suffered the effects of the fall of mankind.

Paul continues, "The good that I wish, I do not do; but I practice the very evil that I do not wish. But if I am doing the very thing I do not wish, I am no longer the one doing it, but sin which dwells in me. . . . I find then the principle that evil is present in me, the one who wishes to do good. For I joyfully concur with the law of God in the inner man, but I see a different law in the members of my body, waging war against the law of my mind, and making me a prisoner of the law of sin which is in my members" (vv. 19-23). Paul repeatedly identified the source of the problem as his flesh, his body, his bodily members. In verse 24 he calls his body "the body of this death." In verse 25 he says that with his flesh he serves the law of sin. All those expressions refer to his unredeemed humanness. The authority and dominion of sin is broken in the believer's life, but sin is still present.

God has planted the incorruptible seed of eternal life deep in the believer's soul. The believer has the power to do what is right because he has a new heart and the presence of the Spirit, who is the down payment, the first installment, on the perfection he will enjoy in the future. Every believer eagerly awaits the day when that perfection is his. Romans 8:23 says, "We ourselves, having the first fruits of the Spirit [having received the down payment of the Spirit and new life], even we ourselves groan within ourselves, waiting eagerly for our adoption as sons, the redemption of our body." We have had a taste of what redemption is like, and therefore we want to be completely redeemed.

Review

I. WHAT HEAVEN IS (see pp. 13-20)

II. WHERE HEAVEN IS (see pp. 28-30)

III. WHAT HEAVEN IS LIKE (see pp. 30-53)

Lesson

IV. WHAT WE WILL BE LIKE

A. A Perfected Soul

Sin has crippled our souls and marred our spirits. It has scarred our thoughts, wills, and emotions. We yearn for the day when the eternal seed within us will bloom into fullness, and we will be completely redeemed.

1. Required

In heaven our souls and bodies will be eternally perfect. We will lose all traces of human fallenness. In fact, no one will enter heaven or dwell there who isn't absolutely perfect. Revelation 6:11 says, "There was given to each of them [those martyred during the Tribulation] a white robe; and they were told that they should rest for a little while longer, until the number of their fellow servants and their brethren who were to be killed even as they had been, should be completed also." The white robes symbolize holiness, purity, and absolute perfection. In Revelation 7:14 one of the elders says, "These are the ones coming out of the great tribulation, and they have washed their robes and made them white in the blood of the Lamb." Again the Bible is emphasizing the perfection of those who enter heaven.

As believers we have within us the seed of perfection, but our souls are not yet perfect. Our bodies aren't the only culprit; our minds, wills, and emotions sin also because our souls are not yet perfected. But the moment a believer dies, his soul is instantly perfected, and he enters God's presence. The body goes to the grave, and the soul goes immediately to heaven. Paul said, "To be absent from the body" is "to be at home with the Lord" (2 Cor. 5:8). In Philippians 1:23 Paul says he has "the desire to depart and be with Christ, for that is very much better."

All the saints who have died are now in heaven without their bodies. Hebrews 12:22 makes that clear: "You have come to Mount Zion, and to the city of the living God, the heavenly Jerusalem, and to myriads of angels, to the general assembly and church of the first-born who are enrolled in heaven, and to God, the Judge of all, and to *the spirits* of righteous men made perfect" (emphasis added).

2. Described

What will the perfected soul be like? God will be able to scrutinize the soul and find no imperfection or sin. First Corinthians 2 gives us further insight: "Who among men knows the thoughts of a man except the spirit of the man, which is in him? Even so the thoughts of God no one knows except the Spirit of God. Now we have received, not the spirit of the world, but the Spirit who is from God, that we might know the things freely given to us by God, which things we also speak, not in words taught by human wisdom, but in those taught by the Spirit, combining spiritual thoughts with spiritual words" (vv. 11-13). Paul is saying that it is impossible to understand who we are in Christ apart from the instruction of the Spirit. We can assume it is also impossible to know what we will be in the future apart from what the Spirit teaches us. And the Spirit says little except to speak of the refer to the "Things which eye has not seen and ear has not heard, and which have not entered the heart of man, all that God has prepared for those who love Him" (1 Cor. 2:9).

a) Negatively

We will experience perfect freedom from evil forever. We will never have a selfish thought or utter useless

59

words. We will never perform an unkind deed or do anything but that which is absolutely righteous, holy, and perfect before God. Can you imagine yourself behaving in such an incredible way? No imperfection will exist in heaven! Revelation 21:27 says, "Nothing unclean and no one who practices abomination and lying, shall ever come into it." No one who has any stain will ever enter the heavenly city. Revelation 22:14-15 says, "Blessed are those who wash their robes, that they may have the right to the tree of life, and may enter by the gates into the city. Outside are the dogs and the sorcerers and the immoral persons and the murderers and the idolaters, and everyone who loves and practices lying."

There will be no sin, suffering, sorrow, or pain in heaven. We will never doubt God or fear His displeasure because we will never do anything to displease Him. No temptation will exist there, because the world, the flesh, and the devil will all be conspicuously absent. Nor will there be persecution, division, disunity, or hate. Quarrels and disagreements will not occur in heaven. No one will be disappointed. Prayer, fasting, repentance, and confession of sin will cease because the need for them will cease. There will be no weeping in heaven because nothing will make us sad. Nor will teaching or evangelism be necessary.

b) Positively

(1) Perfect pleasure

Psalm 16:11 says, "In Thy presence is fullness of joy; in Thy right hand there are pleasures forever." In God's presence will be perfect pleasure.

(2) Perfect knowledge

In 1 Corinthians 13:12 Paul says, "Then I shall know fully just as I also have been fully known." We are known comprehensively, and we'll know comprehensively.

(3) Perfect comfort

We will never experience one uncomfortable moment. In Luke 16:25 Abraham says to the rich
man, "Child, remember that during your life you
received your good things, and likewise Lazarus
[the beggar] bad things, but now he is being comforted here, and you are in agony." Hell is agony;
heaven is eternal comfort.

(4) Perfect love

First Corinthians 13:13 says, "Now abide faith,
hope, love, these three; but the greatest of these
is love." We will love everyone perfectly and will
be loved perfectly. John 13:1 says that Christ
loved His disciples to the end—to perfection.
That's exactly the way we will love. And God will
love us. The love that wept and bled and died on
our behalf will engulf us forever.

(5) Perfect joy

We could summarize by saying that heaven is a
place of unending joy. Joy in this life is always
mixed with sorrow, discouragement, disappoint-
ment, or worry. Sin, grief, and sorrow dampen
all our joys. An honest look at our world's condi-
tion produces only tears. But heaven will be a
place of unmixed joy.

In Matthew 25 the Lord tells the parable about a
man about to go on a journey. He called "his own
slaves, and entrusted his possessions to them.
And to one he gave five talents, to another, two,
and to another, one, each according to his own
ability; and he went on his journey. Immediately
the one who had received the five talents went
and traded with them, and gained five more talents. In the same manner the one who had received the two talents gained two more. But he
who received the one talent went away and dug
in the ground, and hid his master's money" (vv.

61

14-18). The parable is discussing spiritual privileges. Some men use their spiritual privileges, and they are blessed. Others waste those privileges.

One day the master returned and settled accounts with his slaves. "The one who had received the five talents came up and brought five more talents, saying, 'Master, you entrusted five talents to me; see, I have gained five more talents.' His master said to him, 'Well done, good and faithful slave; you were faithful with a few things, I will put you in charge of many things, enter into the joy of your master' " (vv. 20-21). The one who had received the two talents had earned two more. To him the master said, "Well done, good and faithful slave; you were faithful with a few things, I will put you in charge of many things; enter into the joy of your master" (v. 23). The one who wasted his spiritual privilege lost what he had and was cast "into the outer darkness," where there is no joy, but "weeping and gnashing of teeth" (v. 30).

The dominant characteristic of heaven is joy, which springs from all the other features of heaven. Any joy we experience now is merely a taste of what awaits us. In the simplest terms we may accurately define heaven as a place of unmixed and unending joy. Heaven's joy has to be unending because the conditions that produce unmixed joy never change. Heavenly perfection is never altered. Hell is the opposite—it is a place of unmixed and unending pain and torment. But in heaven all the longings of the redeemed soul will be satisfied eternally, and the soul will be perfected forever.

B. A Perfected Body

God made us body and soul—we consist of an inner man and an outer man (Gen. 2:7). Therefore our ultimate perfection demands that both body and soul be renewed. Even the creation of a new heaven and earth demands that we have bodies—a real earth calls for its inhabitants to have real bodies.

1. The promise of resurrection

Death brings about separation. Our bodies go to the grave, and our spirits go to the Lord. That separation continues until the resurrection "in which all who are in the tombs shall hear His voice, and shall come forth; those who did the good deeds to a resurrection of life, those who committed the evil deeds to a resurrection of judgment" (John 5:28-29). Today the souls of believers who have died are in heaven, and the souls of unbelievers who have died are in hell. But one day the bodies of the redeemed will be resurrected and joined to their spirits, and they will enjoy the eternal perfection of body and soul. One day the bodies of the ungodly will be raised from the graves and joined to their spirits, so that both their bodies and souls will endure the torments of hell forever.

Revelation 20:11-15 discusses the resurrection of the ungodly. Verses 13-14 say, "The sea gave up the dead which were in it, and death and Hades [the grave] gave up the dead which were in them; and they were judged, every one of them according to their deeds. And death and Hades were thrown into the lake of fire." One day a resurrection unto damnation and judgment will occur.

As Christians we eagerly await the redemption of our bodies (Rom. 8:23), for what 2 Corinthians 5:1 calls "a house not made with hands, eternal in the heavens." First Thessalonians 4 describes the believers' resurrection: "We do not want you to be uninformed, brethren, about those who are asleep, that you may not grieve, as do the rest who have no hope. For if we believe that Jesus died and rose again, even so God will bring with Him those who have fallen asleep in Jesus. For this we say to you by the word of the Lord, that we who are alive, and remain until the coming of the Lord, shall not precede those who have fallen asleep. For the Lord Himself will descend from heaven with a shout, with the voice of the archangel, and with the trumpet of God; and the dead in Christ shall rise first. Then we who are alive and remain shall be caught up together with them in the clouds to meet the Lord in the air, and thus we shall always be with the Lord" (vv. 13-17). At the rapture, the event Paul is describing in 1 Thessalonians 4, first those believers who are dead will be united with their perfected bodies, then those who are still alive will be caught up and changed. Every Christian still living on the earth when Christ comes will be perfected at the rapture.

We can look forward to the promise of God: a glorified body as well as a glorified spirit. In 2 Corinthians 5:1 Paul says our earthly tent will be torn down, and we will receive a building from God.

2. The body of resurrection

First Corinthians 15 is the definitive chapter on bodily resurrection.

a) Its distinctiveness

Paul said, "Someone will say, 'How are the dead raised? And with what kind of body do they come?' You fool!" (vv. 35-36). That is a severe rebuke. He then goes on to explain himself.

(1) Illustrated by the death of a seed

In verses 36-38 Paul says, "That which you sow does not come to life unless it dies; and that which you sow, you do not sow the body which is to be, but a bare grain, perhaps of wheat or of something else. But God gives it a body just as He wished, and to each of the seeds a body of its own." A seed bears no resemblance to the plant it will produce. The life principle is in the seed, but if you had not previously seen the plant it produced, you would not have known what kind of plant the seed would produce. A seed falls to the ground, decomposes, and then gives life. Similarly our bodies will die, be placed in a grave, and then be raised, just as a seed dies and produces a plant. Our resurrection bodies will be similar to

64

the one that was buried—but also different. We will be ourselves, but we'll also be perfect. The decomposition of the body isn't an obstacle to the resurrection. Just as a seed decomposes and brings forth life, the resurrection body will come from the death of the original body.

(2) Illustrated by the differing animal bodies

In verse 39 Paul says, "All flesh is not the same flesh, but there is one flesh of men, and another flesh of beasts, and another flesh of birds, and another of fish." The flesh of animals is determined by amino acids, of which a myriad of combinations exist. Each combination of amino acids produces a certain kind of flesh. We always produce our own flesh regardless of what we eat. If I were to eat chicken constantly, I wouldn't grow feathers, because the amino acids in my body will only reproduce my own flesh. The amino-acid structure that God put into flesh keeps it distinct. God wasn't restricted to one kind of flesh in creation, Paul argues; why therefore should God be restricted to one kind of flesh in resurrection? We cannot fully understand what the resurrected body will be like, just as those who are familiar only with the flesh of birds cannot fully understand horses.

(3) Illustrated by the differing celestial bodies

In verse 40 Paul says, "There are also heavenly bodies and earthly bodies, but the glory of the heavenly is one, and the glory of the earthly is another." Since God made everything from a tiny, crawling bug to a massive sun, He can make any kind of body He wants. Verse 41 says, "There is one glory of the sun, and another glory of the moon, and another glory of the stars; for star differs from star in glory." No two trees or seeds on earth are exactly alike; no two animals are exactly alike; no two people are exactly alike; no two celestial bodies are exactly alike. Nevertheless, some people still question God's ability to create a resurrection body.

Verse 42 says, "So also is the resurrection of the dead." Nature and astronomy illustrate that God can make any kind of body He wants. As one body differs from another, so the resurrection body can differ from what we now know. God may well create a unique body that preserves our personality distinctions in a state of eternal perfection. The graveyards of men are the seed plots of resurrection.

b) Its characteristics

The resurrection body "is sown a perishable body, it is raised an imperishable body; it is sown in dishonor, it is raised in glory; it is sown in weakness, it is raised in power; it is sown a natural body, it is raised a spiritual body" (vv. 42-44).

(1) Imperishable

Our heavenly bodies will be imperishable—they will never decay. They will be permanently and eternally perfect. You will never look at your hand and notice something you haven't noticed before. You will never notice a lump growing beneath the skin. No X-rays for cancer will exist in heaven, for no one will develop disease there. Absolute, imperishable perfection will be present in heaven.

(2) Glorious

Our bodies will also be glorious, reflecting the glory of God.

(3) Powerful

Paul said our bodies will be raised in power. Our bodies will have abilities beyond imagination to accomplish everything we desire.

(4) Spiritual

Our bodies will be spiritual in the sense that they will give expression to a perfect spirit. Those bodies will be adapted for living in heaven, an existence we know little about.

(5) Christlike

Verse 45 takes us further by saying, "It is written, 'The first man, Adam, became a living soul.' The last Adam [Christ] became a life-giving spirit." Paul contrasts the heads of two families. Adam sinned and brought death on the human race; Jesus Christ brought life. Verses 46-49 say, "The spiritual is not first, but the natural; then the spiritual. The first man is from the earth, earthy; the second man is from heaven. As is the earthy, so also are those who are earthy; and as is the heavenly, so also are those who are heavenly. And just as we have borne the image of the earthy, we shall also bear the image of the heavenly." Just as we are like Adam now, in heaven we will be like Jesus Christ, who is incorruptible, eternal, glorified, powerful, and spiritual—His perfect spirit expresses itself through His glorified humanity. According to Philippians 3:21, God will transform our bodies "into conformity with the body of His [Christ's] glory." Romans 8:29 says we are "predestined to become conformed to the image of His Son." First John 3:2 says, "We know that, when He appears, we shall be like Him, because we shall see Him just as He is."

The best picture of what we'll be like in heaven is Jesus Christ after His resurrection. In His glorified body Christ ascended to heaven (Acts 1:9). After His resurrection He suddenly appeared in rooms where all the doors were shut (John 20:19, 26). He ate with the disciples on several occasions (Luke 24:42-43; John 21:12-14). Revelation 22:2 says that fruit-bearing trees will be in heaven. In the same way, just as Christ ate after His resurrection although He didn't need to, so in eternity we will eat the fruit of heavenly trees, not because we need to but for enjoyment.

We will have bodies fit for the full life of God to indwell and express itself forever. We will be able to eat but will not need to. We will be able to move rapidly through space and matter. We will be ageless and not know pain, tears, sorrow, sickness, or death. We will have bodies of splendor. In a promise to the Old Testament saints, the Lord compared our glorified bodies to the shining of the moon and stars (Dan. 12:3). Christ's glorified body is described as shining like the sun in its strength (Rev. 1:16).

Conclusion

Our longing for heaven should be intense. Finding joy and comfort in this life is irrational, because it idolizes a sin-filled, decaying world and contradicts God's goal, which is to make us like Christ in heaven. If we want to cling to this world and its comforts and accumulate our treasure here, we are irrational and sinful. Furthermore, by seeking what will never satisfy, we are aggravating our misery.

We fear pain, suffering, and death—God has built that reaction into us. But it is unreasonable and even sinful to fear the result of death. I'm not longing to die, but I am longing for what death brings. We should desire heaven like a prisoner longs for freedom, like a sick man longs for health, like the hungry and thirsty long for food and water. If we don't, something is wrong. We should be saying with the apostle John, "Come, Lord Jesus" (Rev. 22:20).

Christians enjoy the best of life and will live eternally with God. All that is glorious, all that is noble, and all that is blessed awaits us in heaven. I hope you are headed to heaven and that your heart yearns for reunion with Christ.

Focusing on the Facts

1. What is the purpose of salvation (see p. 56)?
2. What is the problem the believer faces? Explain (see p. 56).
3. What does Paul mean by "flesh" (see p. 57)?
4. What do the white robes symbolize in Revelation 6:11 (see p. 58)?
5. The moment a believer dies, his soul is _____ _____, and he enters God's _____ (see pp. 58-59).
6. Explain what Revelation 21:27 and 22:14-15 teach about heaven (see p. 60).
7. Describe the perfections of heaven (see pp. 60-62).
8. How can we accurately define heaven in its simplest terms (see p. 62)?
9. What demands that our ultimate perfection be both body and soul (see p. 62)?
10. What passage indicates that the bodies of believers and unbelievers will be resurrected (see p. 63)?
11. Explain the three ways Paul illustrates the distinctiveness of our resurrected bodies (see pp. 64-66).
12. What are the characteristics of our perfected bodies? Explain (see pp. 66-68).
13. Explain 1 Corinthians 15:46-49 (see p. 67).
14. What is the best picture of what we will be like in heaven (see p. 67)?

Pondering the Principles

1. Too often Christians use their humanness as an excuse for sin. They ignore their own obvious violations of God's law, reminding themselves that none of us will be perfect until we arrive in heaven. Although that is true, we are not excused from striving toward that goal. Have you been using the "flesh" as an excuse for your sin? Have you avoided taking responsibility for your violations of God's law? Take time now to meditate on Proverbs 28:13 and Matthew 5:48.

2. According to 1 Thessalonians 4:13 and 18, God communicates the truth of the resurrection to comfort believers who have ex-

perienced the death of believing friends and family. Are you struggling over the death of someone you love? Read God's comfort to you in 1 Thessalonians 4:13-18, and thank Him for His love and tenderness in providing it. Has someone you know recently experienced the death of a believing friend or family member? Read 1 Thessalonians 4:18, and obey its exhortation.

5
Looking Toward Heaven—Part 5
How We Will Relate to One Another

Outline

Introduction

Review
I. What Heaven Is
II. Where Heaven Is
III. What Heaven Is Like
IV. What We Will Be Like

Lesson
V. How We Will Relate to One Another
  A. Our Relation to Angels
    1. Communing with them
    2. Rejoicing with them
    3. Worshiping with them
    4. Being served by them
  B. Our Relation to Family
    1. 1 Corinthians 7
    2. Matthew 22
  C. Our Relation to Other Believers
    1. Unchanged identity
    2. Loving reunion
Conclusion

Introduction

American humorist Mark Twain had a cynical view of life. At the beginning of the third chapter of *The Tragedy of Pudd'nhead Wilson* (1894), he wrote, "Whoever has lived long enough to find out what life is, knows how deep a debt of gratitude we owe to Adam, the first benefactor of our race. He brought death into the world." Reportedly Twain also quipped on one occasion, "You take heaven; I'd rather go to Bermuda." That statement demonstrates a shallow, short-sighted treatment of eternity.

Such a view goes against the grain of the human heart. Ecclesiastes 3:11 says that God has set eternity in the hearts of men. Man yearns for an afterlife and generally finds it difficult, if not impossible, to believe that he ceases to exist after this life. Only the cynic sees life as nothing but a mistake, a failure, and pure foolishness. We who know and love the Lord Jesus Christ have hope.

Since our hope is in heaven, the church needs to return to focusing on it. Our modern, self-indulgent life-style has affected us. As society has made our lives here more comfortable, our longing for the life to come has abated. The subjects of heaven and hell often go unmentioned in the pulpit and on the printed page. During the last fifteen years the only people who seem to have interest in the life to come are those involved in cults, Eastern religions, psychic circles, or those who have made studies of near-death experiences. A deluge of books has been written about such experiences, describing mystical lights, tunnels, and floating sensations, but they seem to relate more to the psychic and occult world than to the church of Jesus Christ.

Our world population is now more than five billion. The United Nations has estimated that about 11 percent of the population dies each year, which means more than fifty million people will die this year. Today alone over 130 thousand people will go either to heaven or to hell. Tomorrow another 130 thousand will follow. For the most part people seem unconcerned and uninterested in such a reality. But in the heart of every individual is a sense of the impending reality of death. The purpose of this study on heaven is to bring about in you an excitement over heaven's realities beyond death. We need to set our affections on things above—to accumulate our treasure in heaven, not on earth.

Review

Lesson

V. HOW WE WILL RELATE TO ONE ANOTHER

A. Our Relation to Angels

Martin Luther believed that an angel is a spiritual creature without a body created by God for the service of Christendom and the church. Angels attend to the presence of God. Since God is in heaven, angels are there as well. God is often called the Lord of hosts, a title that refers to His being surrounded by His holy angels. God always has holy angels in His presence. First Thessalonians 4:17 says that we will always be with the Lord; therefore, we will be with the angels, too. But how will we interact with them?

1. Communing with them

Hebrews 12:22 says, "You have come to Mount Zion and to the city of the living God, the heavenly Jerusalem, and to myriads of angels." "Myriads" refers to an innumerable number. When we enter the heavenly Jerusalem, we will be in the company of the angels and "the general assembly and church of the first-born who are enrolled in heaven, and to God, the Judge of all, and to the spirits of righteous men made perfect, and to Jesus, the mediator of a new covenant" (v. 23). The elect angels and the elect saints form the elect company of inhabitants in the new heaven and earth.

Angels are spirit beings. They do not have bodies, although they can and do take human form when God desires. Some do not understand how we in glorified bodies will be able to interact with spirit beings. But we interact over the telephone with people we cannot see. In heaven we will be able to perceive what to us in the physical world is now invisible.

2. Rejoicing with them

Some Christians wonder if the angels, who have exclusively enjoyed heaven and doing the work of God, will be jealous when we are perfected. But there cannot be a war between glorified saints and elect angels because both are absolutely and eternally holy.

In Luke 15 the three great parables about the lost coin, lost sheep, and the lost son illustrate the heart of God. When the man found his lost sheep, he called "together his friends and his neighbors, saying to them, 'Rejoice with me, for I have found my sheep which was lost!' " (v. 6). Then Christ gave the point of the story: "I tell you that in the same way, there will be more joy in heaven over one sinner who repents, than over ninety-nine righteous persons who need no repentance" (v. 7). God and His holy angels rejoice over the repentance of a sinner.

In the second parable a woman lost a coin. When she found it, she called "together her friends and neighbors, saying, 'Rejoice with me' " (v. 9). In verse 10 Christ says, "In the same way, I tell you, there is joy in the presence of the angels of God over one sinner who repents." Here we find the angels rejoicing. They are not jealous of the redeemed church; they rejoice over it. The story of the prodigal son also depicts that truth. The story ends with the father's saying to his other son, "We had to be merry and rejoice, for this brother of yours was dead and has begun to live, and was lost and has been found" (v. 32). All the servants of the father were called to the feast and rejoiced with him. Those three parables show that God and the angels rejoice over the conversion of sinners. And if they rejoice over our conversion, how much more will they rejoice over us when

74

in perfected souls and bodies we become the epitome of what God began in our redemption.

To the angels we will be a source of eternal joy. They will love us. They will be thrilled with what has been done to perfect us and bring us to the holy presence of the God they worship and adore.

3. Worshiping with them

Revelation 4 explains that we will join the angels in worshiping God. Verse 4 says, "Around the throne were twenty-four thrones; and upon the thrones I saw twenty-four elders sitting, clothed in white garments, and golden crowns on their heads." I believe the twenty-four elders symbolize the church. Some argue that twelve represent Old Testament saints, each from a different tribe, and that twelve are the apostles representing New Testament saints. But regardless, the elders refer to redeemed saints.

Verse 6 says, "Before the throne there was, as it were, a sea of glass like crystal; and in the center and around the throne, four living creatures full of eyes in front and behind." Those creatures, resembling the ones in Ezekiel 1, are angels. They, along with the twenty-four elders, representing redeemed men, cry, " 'Holy, holy, holy, is the Lord God, the Almighty, who was and who is and who is to come.' And when the living creatures give glory and honor and thanks to Him who sits on the throne, to Him who lives forever and ever, the twenty-four elders will fall down before Him who sits on the throne, and will worship Him who lives forever and ever, and will cast their crowns before the throne saying, 'Worthy art Thou, our Lord and our God' " (vv. 8-11).

Revelation 5:8-9 portrays a similar scene: "The four living creatures and the twenty-four elders fell down before the Lamb, having each one a harp, and golden bowls full of incense, which are the prayers of the saints. And they sang a new song, saying, 'Worthy art Thou.' " They are singing to the glory of Christ. The apostle John interjects, "I looked, and I heard the voice of many angels around the throne and the living creatures and the elders; and the number of them was myriads of myriads, and thousands of thousands, saying with a loud voice, 'Worthy is the Lamb that was slain' " (v. 11). Verse 13 says that "every created thing which is in heaven and on the earth and under the earth and on the sea, and all things in them, I heard saying, 'To Him who sits on the throne, and to the Lamb, be blessing and honor and glory and dominion forever and ever.' " We will praise and worship God with the angels forever.

4. Being served by them

Hebrews 1:14 says of angels, "Are they not all ministering spirits, sent out to render service for the sake of those who will inherit salvation?" Angels are ministering spirits whose duty is to serve the heirs of salvation. In Hebrews 1 they are contrasted with Christ: Christ's destiny is to reign, angels' is to serve. They were created to serve the redeemed not merely in time but also in eternity. We will reign with Christ, and those who serve Christ will serve us.

Hebrews 2:7 says that God "made [Christ] for a little while lower than the angels." That happened in His incarnation, when He humbled Himself and died the ignominious death of the cross. But He was made lower than angels only for a little while, then was exalted and crowned with glory and honor. Now Christ reigns. Likewise, we are lower than the angels only for a little while. When we enter heaven, we will reign with Jesus Christ. Ephesians 1:21 says that Christ is head over "all rule and authority and power and dominion"—a reference to angelic beings.

In Revelation 3:21 Christ says, "He who overcomes, I will grant to him to sit down with Me on My throne, as I also overcame and sat down with My Father on His throne." God has promised that we will sit on the throne with Christ at God's right hand. We will reign; angels will serve. Hebrews 1:13 says, "To which of the angels has He ever said, 'Sit at My right hand, until I make Thine enemies a footstool for Thy feet'?" We will commune with angels, rejoice with them, and praise

God with them, but we will rule over them. They will serve us in heaven.

First Corinthians 6:1 says, "Does any one of you, when he has a case against his neighbor, dare to go to law before the unrighteous, and not before the saints?" Paul was telling the Corinthians not to sue other believers in a secular court. He continued, "Do you not know that the saints will judge the world? And if the world is judged by you, are you not competent to constitute the smallest law courts?" (v. 2). When Christ establishes His earthly kingdom, believers will be His ambassadors, rulers, kings, and princes. We will carry out the verdicts of Christ. Verse 3 goes further: "Do you not know that we shall judge [lit., "rule" or "govern"] angels?" Throughout eternity, angels will serve us as we rule with Christ. They will do what we ask them to do in joyful expression of their intended purpose.

B. Our Relation to Family

People often ask me, "Will I be married to the same woman in heaven?" Some say, "I don't want to lose my wife; I can't imagine going to heaven and not being married." Will we have family love and fellowship? Will our relationships in heaven be like they are here? When considering those questions, it is important to remember that we will all be perfect. No one will ever do, say, or think anything wrong.

1. 1 Corinthians 7

Scripture speaks specifically to the issue of marriage and family in 1 Corinthians 7. Paul said, "This I say, brethren, the time [of the Lord's arrival] has been shortened, so that from now on both those who have wives should be as though they had none; and those who weep, as though they did not weep; those who rejoice, as though they did not rejoice; and those who buy, as though they did not possess; and those who use the world, as though they did not make full use of it; for the form [Gk., schēma] of this world is passing away" (vv. 29-31). In the context Paul lists some of the things that are passing away: marriage, weeping, earthly rejoicing, and

77

ownership. All the *schēma* of the world is passing away. *Schēma* refers to fashion, manner of life, and a way of doing things.

Paul was saying we should take what life brings, yet keep from being engulfed in it because all those things are part of a *schēma* that is temporary. Although the responsibilities of marriage are wonderful, don't allow your marriage to become an excuse for your failure to serve God, put treasure in heaven, or set your affections on things above. We should experience sorrow and joy and buy what we need to buy, but we must not let our emotions and possessions control us so that we become entangled by this passing world.

Verses 32-33 say, "One who is unmarried is concerned about the things of the Lord, how he may please the Lord; but one who is married is concerned about the things of the world, how he may please his wife." If you can remain single, do. Concentrate on the things of the Lord because marriage is a temporary provision. That does not mean we are to become indifferent to our marriages. God has given us a wonderful gift in the present scheme of things, and we need to enjoy our marriages to the fullest. Marriage is a grace of life (1 Pet. 3:7). However, we are to keep marriage in perspective—to recognize that it is passing away.

2. Matthew 22

Verse 23 says, "Some Sadducees (who say there is no resurrection) came to Him [Jesus] and questioned Him." The Pharisees taught that after the resurrection each person would have the same relationships he has here. He would be married to the same woman and have the same family forever. They believed the next life would be exactly like this one. But the Sadducees did not believe a resurrection would occur, and therefore they tried to paint an absurd portrait of the Pharisees' theology in the guise of asking Jesus a question.

They said, "Teacher, Moses said, 'If a man dies, having no children, his brother as next of kin shall marry his wife, and raise up an offspring to his brother' " (v. 24).

78

That's a Mosaic principle taught in Deuteronomy 25. Next the Sadducees presented their hypothetical scenario: " 'There were seven brothers with us; and the first married and died, and having no offspring left his wife to his brother; so also the second, and the third, down to the seventh. And last of all, the woman died. In the resurrection therefore whose wife of the seven shall she be? For they all had her.' But Jesus answered and said to them, 'You are mistaken, not understanding the Scriptures, or the power of God. For in the resurrection they neither marry, nor are given in marriage, but are like angels in heaven' " (vv. 25-30). All the angels were created at one time, and angels don't procreate. Christ's words teach that men here will be men in eternity, and women here will be women in eternity, but there will be no marrying or giving in marriage in heaven. In that way we will be like the angels.

Why will there be no marriage in heaven? Because it won't be needed. God created marriage because man needed a helper, woman needed a protector, and together both were to produce children. In heaven, man won't need a helper because he will be perfect. Woman won't need a protector because she will be perfect. And no one will be born in heaven because only the redeemed can live there. Someone might be thinking, *But I'm happily married. I love my wife. She's my best friend and my dearest companion in every area of life.* That's good! You will enjoy that companionship with her in heaven forever—and with every other person in heaven as well. If having such a deep relationship with your spouse here is so wonderful, imagine how wonderful to enjoy the best of human relationships, glorified to the point that you enjoy the same relationship equally with every human being.

C. Our Relation to Other Believers

1. Unchanged identity

We will be forever who we are now. Genesis 25:8 says, "Abraham breathed his last and died in a ripe old age, an old man and satisfied with life; and he was gathered to his people" (cf. Genesis 35:29; 49:29; Numbers 20:24;

Judges 2:10). Often when a person died, the biblical writers said he was gathered to his people, implying that those who died maintained their identities—they went to their people.

In 2 Samuel 12 David's child died. In verse 23 David says, "Now he has died; why should I fast? Can I bring him back again? I shall go to him, but he will not return to me." David knew that both he and his child would maintain their identities. In heaven everyone will maintain his identity. We will be a diverse company of individuals.

Also the New Testament illustrates that our identities will be unchanged. While sharing the Passover meal with His disciples, Christ said, "Take this [cup] and share it among yourselves; for I say to you, I will not drink of the fruit of the vine from now on until the Kingdom of God comes" (Luke 22:17-18). Christ was saying that He and His disciples would drink the fruit of the vine together again.

Our Lord, speaking about the millennial kingdom, is even clearer about this issue in Matthew 8:11: "I say to you, that many shall come from east and west, and recline at table with Abraham, and Isaac, and Jacob, in the kingdom of heaven." Abraham, Isaac, and Jacob will be there, and we will too.

Revelation 19 says, " 'Let us rejoice and be glad and give the glory to Him, for the marriage of the Lamb has come and His bride has made herself ready.' And it was given to her to clothe herself in fine linen, bright and clean; for the fine linen is the righteous acts of the saints. . . . 'Blessed are those who are invited to the marriage supper of the Lamb' " (vv. 7-9). A marriage supper in heaven for the Lamb and His bride, the church, will take place. The guests will be the Old Testament and the Tribulation saints. All the redeemed will maintain their identity forever, only in a perfected form. We will be able to have fellowship with Enoch, Noah, Abraham, Jacob, Samuel, Moses, Joshua, Esther, Elijah, Elisha, Isaiah, Daniel, Ezekiel, David, Peter, Barnabas,

Paul, or anyone else we choose, and we all will be ourselves.

The appearance of Moses and Elijah on the Mount of Transfiguration proves that even though they died centuries before, they still maintained their identity (Matt. 17:3). Peter, James, and John recognized them (v. 4), which implies that we will be able to recognize people we've never seen before. We will instantly know everyone and enjoy their company, never ceasing to be who we are. Jesus told the thief on the cross, "Today you shall be with Me in Paradise" (Luke 23:43). They reached heaven together as distinct persons.

When the Sadducees tried to trap Jesus about the resurrection, He cited Exodus 3:6: "I am the God . . . of Abraham, the God of Isaac, and the God of Jacob," commenting, "God is not the God of the dead but of the living" (Matt. 22:32). Christ meant that Abraham, Isaac, and Jacob were still living and that God continued to rule over them, not merely in the past. In Luke 16 the rich man died and went to hell. The beggar Lazarus died and went to heaven. Both maintained their identities, and so will we.

Revelation 2:17 says, "To him who overcomes . . . I will give . . . a new name." In heaven our identities will not change, but our names will. Revelation 3:5 adds, "He who overcomes shall thus be clothed in white garments; and I will not erase his name from the book of life, and I will confess his name before My Father." Christ will confess our perfected, eternal names before God. Verse 12 continues, "He who overcomes, I will make him a pillar in the temple of My God, and he will not go out from it anymore; and I will write upon him the name of My God, and the name of the city of My God, the new Jerusalem, which comes down out of heaven from My God, and My new name." Every believer will be in heaven, genuinely bearing the name of God and Christ.

2. Loving reunion

People often ask if we will be reunited with our family and friends in heaven. That each person will retain his identity implies we will be reunited with them. In fact, after 1 Thessalonians 4:13-17 promises the rapture of the church, verse 18 says, "Comfort one another with these words." That comfort comes from the prospect of reunion. Some Thessalonian believers feared that those who had died might miss the rapture. Paul encouraged those fearful believers to comfort one another, assuring them that those who had died would not miss His coming. Christ will come, bringing believers who have died with Him, and will give them and those who are alive glorified bodies. We will all be together forever from then on. Since we will know everyone, we will therefore know our loved ones.

In Revelation 21:1-4 John says, "I saw a new heaven and a new earth; for the first heaven and the first earth passed away, and there is no longer any sea. And I [John] saw the holy city, new Jerusalem, coming down out of heaven from God, made ready as a bride adorned for her husband. And I heard a loud voice from the throne, saying, 'Behold, the tabernacle of God is among men, and He shall dwell among them, and they shall be His people, and God Himself shall be among them, and He shall wipe away every tear from their eyes; and there shall no longer be any death; there shall no longer be any mourning, or crying, or pain.' " Fellowship will exist without tears, separation, pain, death, sorrow, or anxiety. The things that make fellowship difficult on earth will all be removed. We will have relationships such as we have never experienced. Beauty will be abundant in heaven. Perfect humor will also exist in heaven because that, too, is a gift from God.

Conclusion

Theologian A. A. Hodge wrote, "Heaven, as the eternal home of the divine Man and of all the redeemed members of the human race, must necessarily be thoroughly human in its structure, conditions, and activities. Its joys and its occupations must all be rational, moral, emotional, voluntary, and active. There must be the exercise of all faculties, the gratification of all tastes, the development of all talent capacities, the realization of all ideals. The reason, the intellectual curiosity, the imagination, the aesthetic instincts, the holy affections, the social affinities, the inexhaustible resources of strength and power native to the human soul, must all find in heaven exercise and satisfaction" (*Evangelical Theology* [Carlisle, Pa.: Banner of Truth, 1976], p. 400).

Is it any wonder that the psalmist said, "Precious in the sight of the Lord is the death of His godly ones" (Ps. 116:15)? Should it surprise us that the apostle Paul said, "Things which eye has not seen and ear has not heard, and which have not entered the heart of man, all that God has prepared for those who love Him" (1 Cor. 2:9)? What a hope we have—glorious relationships await us!

Focusing on the Facts

1. Explain what Ecclesiastes 3:11 is saying (see p. 72).
2. The title "Lord of hosts" refers to what (see p. 73)?
3. The elect _____ and the elect _____ form the elect company of inhabitants in the new heaven and earth (see p. 73).
4. What insight do the parables of Luke 15 give into the angels' attitude toward us (see pp. 74-75)?
5. In general, whom do the twenty-four elders and the four living creatures in Revelation 4 represent (see p. 75)?
6. What does Hebrews 1:14 explain about our relation to angels (see p. 76)?
7. According to Hebrews 2:7, Christ was made "for a little while lower than the angels." When did that happen (see p. 76)?
8. What is the point of 1 Corinthians 6:1-3 (see p. 77)?
9. What does *schēma* mean? Using that definition, explain 1 Corinthians 7:29-31 (see pp. 77-78).
10. What disagreement with the Pharisees sparked the Sadducees' question in Matthew 22 (see p. 78)?
11. Give scriptural support for the assertion that our identities will be unchanged in heaven (see pp. 79-81).
12. Why is Matthew 17:4 significant in light of our discussion on heaven (see p. 81)?
13. Will we be reunited with family and friends in heaven? Explain (see pp. 81-82).

Pondering the Principles

1. Revelation 4-5 stresses that the elect angels and redeemed saints will worship God together. In fact, worship characterizes heaven. Since worship will be such an important part of life in our glorified bodies, it should be a priority now. The Bible constantly reminds us that worship is an earthly responsibility, as well as a heavenly expression. A life filled with worship focuses on God rather than self. Is your life characterized by worship? Or are you self-focused? Begin using a psalm a day as the basis for your prayers, concentrating on the psalmist's attitude of praise and worship.

2. Although this present *schēma* is passing away, our Lord commanded us to be good stewards of that which He committed to us here. Marriage, for example, is a serious responsibility. In fact, our marriages are to be living portraits of Christ's relationship with His church. How well does your marriage picture that relationship? Does your love for your spouse remind those around you of Christ and His Bride? Decide today to renew your efforts at being the right kind of spouse and at reflecting Christlike love to all you see.

6
Looking Toward Heaven—Part 6
How We Will Relate to God

Outline

Review
  I. What Heaven Is
 II. Where Heaven Is
III. What Heaven Is Like
 IV. What We Will Be Like
  V. How We Will Relate to One Another

Lesson
 VI. How We Will Relate to God
    A. Our Fellowship with God
       1. Summarized
       2. Supported
          a) John 17
          b) John 14
          c) Revelation 21
    B. Our Vision of God
       1. Actual observation of Him
          a) Explained
          b) Supported
       2. Spiritual comprehension of Him

Conclusion

Lesson

We have been learning that heaven is the eternal dwelling place of God and all the redeemed of all the ages. Heaven is a place where there is infinite perfection of body and soul, a perfect environment of love, joy, peace, fulfillment, and satisfaction. But now we come to the most glorious reality of heaven—our relationship to God.

VI. HOW WE WILL RELATE TO GOD

A. Our Fellowship with God

The first thing to note is that we will be with Him. Since God is the Supreme Occupant of heaven, being with Him is the supreme joy of heaven. We will have fellowship with the Father and the Lord Jesus Christ.

1. Summarized

First John 1:3 defines salvation as having fellowship with God: "Our fellowship is with the Father, and with His Son Jesus Christ." When we become believers, we enter into communion with God. God's life becomes ours. We become so identified with Him that "the reproaches of those who reproach [Him] have fallen on [us]" (Ps. 69:9). His will becomes our will and His purpose our purpose. Even though sin hinders our walk with Christ on earth, the deepest part of our regenerated souls is united with the living God and in fellowship with the living Christ. Salvation brought us into communion—we can talk and commune with God. We pray to Him. We hear Him speak in the Word. He moves silently and providentially in our lives to reveal Himself. We enjoy spiritual communion with God. But that communion is incomplete. Only when we are in heaven will we enter into full, unhindered fellowship with God.

2. Supported

a) John 17

In His high-priestly prayer in John 17, Christ asks the Father to return Him to the glory He had before the world began. Anticipating the completion of His work on earth, He was eager to rejoin the Father. In verse 24 He prays, "Father, I desire that they also [all who come to believe in Christ], whom Thou hast given Me, be with Me where I am." We often think about how much we long to be with Christ, but must also remember that Christ longs to be with us. In verse 24 Christ supplies the reason for His longing: "that they may behold My glory, which Thou hast given Me." Christ wants us to see His glory—to see Him for who He is. Yet we won't merely see Him; verse 24 says we will be with Him, which implies that we will be participants, not mere spectators.

b) John 14

In John 13:36-38 Jesus says to His disciples, " 'Where I go, you cannot follow Me now [a reference to His impending death]; but you shall follow later.' Peter said to Him, 'Lord, why can I not follow You right now? I will lay down my life for You.' Jesus answered, 'Will you lay down your life for Me? Truly, truly, I say to you, a cock shall not crow, until you deny Me three times.' "

Then in John 14:1 Jesus says, "Let not your heart be troubled." He gave that exhortation because the disciples were troubled at the thought of His leaving them. He was their resource for everything. When

87

they needed comfort, He comforted them. When they needed wisdom, He taught them. When they needed food, He provided it. In the three years they had been together, He had become their very lives. He said, therefore, "Let not your heart be troubled; believe in God, believe also in Me. In My Father's house are many dwelling places; if it were not so, I would have told you; for I go to prepare a place for you" (John 14:1-2). We will be with the Father and with Christ in the Father's house. Everyone in heaven lives in the Father's house. Many houses are not necessary—only the one house, the dwelling place of God.

In verse 3 Jesus says, "If I go and prepare a place for you, I will come again, and receive you to *Myself*" (emphasis added). Simply put, we are going more to a person than to a place. We will enter fellowship with God and His Son, and we will never leave His presence. Being with God is the essence of heaven. Heaven will be paradise regained but infinitely exalted beyond what Adam and Eve experienced in the Garden. We will enjoy unending fellowship with God. Since God is infinitely perfect, we will never grow bored of being with Him. Forever we will experience the unfolding glories of His infinite Person.

c) Revelation 21

In Revelation 21:1-3 John says, "I saw a new heaven and a new earth; for the first heaven and the first earth passed away, and there is no longer any sea. And I saw the holy city, new Jerusalem, coming down out of heaven from God, made ready as a bride adorned for her husband. And I heard a loud voice from the throne, saying, 'Behold, the tabernacle of God is among men, and He shall dwell among them, and they shall be His people, and God Himself shall be among them.' " The expressions "among men" and "among them" speak of God's intimate presence. God Himself will pitch His tent among men and dwell among them. The glory of heaven is that believers will forever enjoy the pleasure of God's company.

B. Our Vision of God

1. Actual observation of Him

   a) Explained

   In heaven we will actually see the Lord. However, you may think of several scriptural statements that seem to contradict that. After all, God said, "No man can see Me and live!" (Ex. 33:20). John 1:18 says that "no man has seen God at any time" (cf. 1 John 4:12). First Timothy 6:16 declares that God alone "possesses immortality and dwells in unapproachable light; whom no man has seen or can see." In Exodus 33 Moses asks God to show him His glory (v. 18). In reply, God explains that He cannot show Moses His full glory, though He will consent to show him His back.

   It is true. God *is* inaccessible to mortal man. Indeed, He is "of purer eyes than to behold evil, and canst not look on iniquity" (Hab. 1:13, KJV*). Therefore, so long as we are tainted by sin, we cannot see God. We will be free from sin in heaven, yet even in heaven we won't see God in His infinity because we will always be finite and therefore incapable of comprehending the infinite. Nevertheless, we will see God in a way we cannot see Him now. Now we see only a glimpse, like the disciples who saw Jesus pull back His veil of flesh on the mount of transfiguration (Matt. 17:1-9). They saw a little glow, but not the full blaze of God's glorious presence. Only a glorified, sinless person could endure that. Since our souls and bodies will be perfect in heaven, we will have a greater capacity to see God's revelation of Himself.

   b) Supported

   Matthew 5:8 says, "Blessed are the pure in heart, for they shall see God." The Greek verb translated "see" (*horaō*) speaks of a future continuous reality in an environment where we are continually seeing God.

*King James Version.

89

Kings of the ancient Orient secluded themselves from their people. To have an audience with a king was a rare privilege. Believers, however, will forever see the King of kings!

The psalmist said, "As the deer pants for the water brooks, so my soul pants for Thee, O God. My soul thirsts for God, for the living God; when shall I come and appear before God?" (Ps. 42:1-2). The psalmist wanted to see God. Philip, speaking for all the disciples, said to Christ, "Show us the Father" (John 14:8). The redeemed have always longed to see God.

In this life we see God not with the physical eye but with the heart and mind. We see Him moving in history and in our individual circumstances. We see Him reflected in His creation, providence, and revelation. We see His grace, mercy, and love revealed in the work of His Spirit. But I believe that in heaven we will see God Himself with our physical eyes. In Exodus 33 God tells Moses that he would be permitted to see His back. Contrast that with Revelation 22:3-5: "There shall no longer be any curse; and the throne of God and of the Lamb shall be in it, and His bond-servants shall serve Him; and *they shall see His face.* . . . The Lord God shall illumine them" (emphasis added). God will reveal the light of His glory, and through perfect eyes we will see the very face of God. God is spirit (John 4:24), and spirit is invisible; therefore, whenever God manifests Himself He does so in the form of light.

2. Spiritual comprehension of Him

I believe that in heaven believers will also see God with the eye of the mind. In other words, we will comprehend God. First Corinthians 13:12 says, "Now we see in a mirror dimly, but then face to face; now I know in part, but then I shall know fully just as I also have been fully known." I believe we will have an instantaneous awareness and knowledge of the fullness of God—as much as human beings have capacity for. So when Christ said, "Blessed are the pure in heart, for they shall

90

see God" (Matt. 5:8), He was referring not only to seeing God with glorified eyes but with glorified minds as well.

We will also see Christ. First John 3:1-2 says, "See how great a love the Father has bestowed upon us, that we should be called children of God; and such we are. For this reason the world does not know us, because it did not know Him. Beloved, now we are children of God, and it has not appeared as yet what we shall be. We know that, when He appears, we shall be like Him, because we shall see Him just as He is." The day is coming when we will see Christ and be like Him. Seeing Christ and the Father will overwhelm and eternally awe us. But understanding that glory will enrapture our minds with delight forever.

Conclusion

David said, "As for me, I will behold thy face in righteousness: I shall be satisfied, when I awake, with thy likeness" (Ps. 17:15, KJV). What really satisfies you? New clothes? A new job? A promotion? A new house or car? A great meal? A fun time? A vacation? David said his ultimate satisfaction would be seeing the face of God and being like Him. As Christians, our ultimate satisfaction should be to know and see our God and His Son, Jesus Christ. Heaven will provide us with that privilege—an undiminished, unwearied sight of His infinite glory and beauty, bringing us infinite and eternal delight. We can understand why Peter wanted to stay on the Mount of Transfiguration (Matt. 17:4)!

In "My Savior First of All" eighteenth-century hymn writer Fanny Crosby wrote:

> When my life work is ended, and I cross the swelling tide,
> When the bright and glorious morning I shall see,
> I shall know my Redeemer when I reach the other side,
> And His smile will be the first to welcome me. . . .

Thru the gates of the city in a robe of spotless
  white,
He will lead me where no tears will ever fall;
In the glad song of ages I shall mingle with delight
But I long to meet my Savior first of all.

Those words have special significance because Fanny Crosby was
blind. When she died, the first person she saw was Jesus Christ.
What will be our relationship to the Lord in heaven? We will see
Him and be with Him. I hope that is your ultimate satisfaction.

Focusing on the Facts

1. How does 1 John 1:3 define salvation (see p. 86)?
2. What presently hinders our communion with God (see p. 86)?
3. According to John 17:24, why does Christ long for us to be with
   Him (see p. 87)?
4. Being with God is the _____ of _____ .
   Explain (see p. 88).
5. What passages seem to contradict the assertion that we will see
   God in heaven? How can we explain those apparent contradic-
   tions (see p. 89)?
6. What cultural insight illuminates Matthew 5:8 (see pp. 89-90)?
7. What does it mean to see God with the mind's eye (see p. 90)?
8. What will happen to believers when they see Jesus Christ (1
   John 3:2; see p. 91)?
9. Explain what should be a believer's ultimate satisfaction (Ps.
   17:15; see pp. 91-92).

Pondering the Principles

1. John 14 reminds us that Christ so longs to be with us that He is
   preparing a place for us. John's reminder should not only make
   us eager for heaven but also motivate us to spend time with the
   Lord now. Have you neglected spending time communing with
   God in His Word and through prayer? Have other people or activities drawn you away from Him? Begin today to reorder your
   time and priorities so that you are doing now what you will do
   for eternity—be with Him.

2. First John 3:1-2 assures us that Christ will come for us. Verse 3 declares the appropriate response to His coming: "Every one who has this hope fixed on Him purifies himself, just as He is pure." Your knowledge of Christ's imminent return should push you toward personal holiness. Pursue a study on personal holiness by tracing the words *holy* and *holiness* through Scripture, and look through books on the subject at your local Christian bookstore or church library.

7
Looking Toward Heaven—Part 7
What We Will Do—Part 1

Outline

Review
   I. What Heaven Is
  II. Where Heaven Is
 III. What Heaven Is Like
 IV. What We Will Be Like
   V. How We Will Relate to One Another
 VI. How We Will Relate to God

Lesson
VII. What We Will Do
  A. Negatively
  B. Positively
    1. Worship
      a) Explained
      b) Illustrated
    2. Reign
      a) A delegated reign
      b) A perfect reign
      c) A promised reign
      d) A proportionate reign

Conclusion

Review

I. WHAT HEAVEN IS (see pp. 13-20)

II. WHERE HEAVEN IS (see pp. 28-30)

III. WHAT HEAVEN IS LIKE (see pp. 30-53)

IV. WHAT WE WILL BE LIKE (see pp. 58-68)

V. HOW WE WILL RELATE TO ONE ANOTHER (see pp. 73-83)

VI. HOW WE WILL RELATE TO GOD (see pp. 86-92)

Lesson

VII. WHAT WE WILL DO

In researching the subject of heaven, I read several books, various journal articles, and a file of information about heaven that I have collected through the years. Discovering what people think heaven is like and what they think we will do there was interesting. Some people suggest that we will sit on the edge of a cloud and play a harp. Others suggest that we will do such things as polish the foundation stones of the New Jerusalem. Some suggest that we won't do anything at all. The early twentieth-century English writer Rudyard Kipling must have had that concept in mind when he wrote the verse "When Earth's Last Picture Is Painted":

> When earth's last picture is painted
> And the tubes are twisted and dried,
> When the oldest colours have faded,
> And the youngest critic has died,
> We shall rest, and faith, we shall need it—
> Lie down for an aeon or two,
> Till the Master of All Good Workmen
> Shall put us to work anew.

Kipling mentions work eventually, but the "aeon or two" of doing nothing bothers me. Kipling's is almost a Rip Van Winkle view of heaven. Will we sleep in heaven? Will we merely loiter there forever? Or will we have something to do—something to plan for, some responsibility to carry out, some goal that will demand all our powers to reach?

A. Negatively

Part of understanding what we will do in heaven is understanding what we will not do. We will not sin; therefore, we will never need to confess sin or struggle with it. We will never need to apologize to anyone. We will never experience guilt. We will never need to write a letter to correct something we said or did. We will not need to straighten out something that got confused, because nothing will ever get confused. We will never need to repair or replace anything, because nothing will malfunction or wear out. We will never need to help anyone because no one will need help. We will never have to battle Satan or the demons. We will never have to deal with sinners. We will never need to defend ourselves against attack because we will never be attacked.

We'll never be sad or lonely. We'll never be hurt emotionally or physically. We'll never need to be cured, counseled, coddled, or entertained. We'll never experience anything but absolute joy. We'll never grieve, because we won't lose anyone or miss anyone. We won't need to be careful, because we will never make a mistake. We won't need to plan for emergencies or avoid danger, because we won't encounter emergencies or danger.

B. Positively

The essence of heaven is experiencing unmixed and unending joy, having a perfect body and soul, and dwelling with the Lamb and the Father in intimate fellowship forever. But what will we *do?* Although the Bible doesn't specify what our individual responsibilities will be, it does provide a general description of our roles.

1. Worship

   a) Explained

   Heaven will be a place of eternal, loving, adoring worship. We will continually praise God without interruption. Our worship will not be related to a particular place, because all heaven will be a temple. In fact, God's purpose in salvation, as clearly delineated in Scripture, was to create an eternal group of worshipers. Speaking to the Samaritan woman, Christ said, "Such people the Father seeks to be His worshipers" (John 4:23). Philippians 3:3 describes Christians as those who "worship in the Spirit of God and glory in Christ Jesus and put no confidence in the flesh." In heaven we will have a fuller knowledge of who God is and whàt He has done than we have now. That deep knowledge of His attributes, deeds, and presence will burst forth in unending praise.

   What thrills me most about our heavenly praise is that it will be perfect. Many times I want to praise God with all my heart, but other thoughts crowd in and clutter my mind. Have you ever been praising God when some evil or trivial thought entered your mind, or some nonsensical notion interrupted your praise? How discouraging to realize how earthbound we are! In heaven our praise will always come out of pure hearts with pure motives and no distractions.

   b) Illustrated

   A quick survey of the book of Revelation will help us grasp the importance of praise in heaven. In Revelation 14:6-7 John says, "I saw another angel flying in midheaven, having an eternal gospel to preach to those who live on the earth, and to every nation and tribe and tongue and people; and he said with a loud voice, 'Fear God, and give Him glory, because the hour of His judgment has come; and worship Him who made the heaven and the earth and sea and springs of water.' " The angel was proclaiming the eternal gospel, the everlasting good news. It was basically a call to reverence, glorify, and worship God. God calls all men to do just that. The gospel is a mandate to praise God.

Revelation 4:10-11, which speaks of events occurring in heaven, says, "The twenty-four elders will fall down before Him who sits on the throne, and will worship Him who lives forever and ever, and will cast their crowns before the throne, saying, 'Worthy art Thou, our Lord and our God, to receive glory and honor and power; for Thou didst create all things, and because of Thy will they existed and were created.' "

In chapter 5 the scene remains in heaven: "When [the Lamb] had taken the book, the four living creatures and the twenty-four elders fell down before the Lamb, having each one a harp, and golden bowls full of incense, which are the prayers of the saints. And they sang a new song, saying, 'Worthy art Thou to take the book, and to break its seals; for Thou wast slain, and didst purchase for God with Thy blood men from every tribe and tongue and people and nation. And Thou hadst made them to be a kingdom and priests to our God; and they will reign upon the earth.' And I looked, and I heard the voice of many angels around the throne and the living creatures and the elders; and the number of them was myriads of myriads [i.e., limitless numbers], and thousands of thousands, saying with a loud voice, 'Worthy is the Lamb that was slain to receive power and riches and wisdom and might and honor and glory and blessing.' And every created thing which is in heaven and on the earth and under the earth and on the sea, and all things in them, I heard saying, 'To Him who sits on the throne, and to the Lamb, be blessing and honor and glory and dominion forever and ever.' And the four living creatures kept saying, 'Amen.' And the elders fell down and worshiped" (vv. 8-14).

Revelation 7 says, "After these things I looked, and behold, a great multitude, which no one could count, from every nation and all tribes and peoples and tongues, standing before the throne and before the Lamb, clothed in white robes, and palm branches were in their hands; and they cry out with a loud voice, saying, 'Salvation to our God who sits on the throne, and to the Lamb.' And all the angels were standing around the throne and around the elders and the four living creatures; and they fell on their faces before the throne and worshiped God, saying, 'Amen, blessing and glory and wisdom and thanksgiving and honor and power and might, be to our God forever and ever, Amen' " (vv. 9-12).

Revelation 11 says, "The seventh angel sounded; and there arose loud voices in heaven, saying, 'The kingdom of the world has become the kingdom of our Lord, and of His Christ; and He will reign forever and ever.' And the twenty-four elders, who sit on their thrones before God, fell on their faces and worshiped God, saying, 'We give Thee thanks, O Lord God, the Almighty, who art and who wast, because Thou hast taken Thy great power and hast begun to reign' " (vv. 15-17).

Revelation 15 says, "I saw, as it were, a sea of glass mixed with fire, and those who had come off victorious from the beast and from his image and from the number of his name, standing on the sea of glass, holding harps of God. And they sang the song of Moses the bond-servant of God and the song of the Lamb, saying, 'Great and marvelous are Thy works, O Lord God, the Almighty; righteous and true are Thy ways, Thou King of the nations. Who will not fear, O Lord, and glorify Thy name? For Thou alone art holy; for all the nations will come and worship before Thee, for Thy righteous acts have been revealed' " (vv. 2-4). Verse 1 refers to such praise as a "sign in heaven."

Revelation 19 begins, "After these things I heard, as it were, a loud voice of a great multitude in heaven, saying, 'Hallelujah! Salvation and glory and power belong to our God; because His judgments are true and righteous; for He has judged the great harlot who was corrupting the earth with her immorality, and He has avenged the blood of His bond-servants on her.' And a second time they said, 'Hallelujah! Her smoke rises up forever and ever' " (vv. 1-3). We will praise God eternally not only for His grace but also for His justice. Verse 4 continues, "The twenty-four elders and the four living creatures fell down, worshiped God who sits on the throne saying, 'Amen. Hallelujah!' And a voice came from the throne, saying, 'Give praise to our God, all you His bond-servants, you who fear Him, the small and the great.' And I heard, as it were, the voice of a great multitude and as the sound of many waters and as the sound of mighty peals of thunder, saying, 'Hallelujah! For the Lord our God, the Almighty, reigns' " (vv. 4-6). In heaven we will be preoccupied with praise. That's a strong reason for being preoccupied with praising God right now.

Perfect praise will be the highest, noblest expression of our perfected being. We will recognize the splendor of God. We will see clearly His majesty. We will see His glory and perfection. And gazing on God's perfections eternally will compel us to offer uninterrupted, unrestrained, adoring, loving worship—it will be our delight!

In *The City of God* Saint Augustine wrote, "How great will be that felicity [joy], where there will be no evil, where no good will be withheld, when there will be leisure for the praises of God, who will be all in all! What other occupation could there be, in a state where there will be no inactivity of idleness, and yet no toil constrained by want? I can think of none" ([Baltimore: Penguin, 1972], p. 1087). We will spend eternity doing what we most desire—praising God.

Professor E. L. Maskell wrote, "The sole justification for praising God is that God is praiseworthy. We do not praise God because it does us good, though no doubt it does. Nor do we praise Him because it does Him good, for in fact it does not. Praise is thus strictly ecstatic in the sense that it takes us wholly out of

101

ourselves; it is purely and solely directed upon God. . . . Praise is entirely directed upon God. It takes our attention entirely off ourself and concentrates it entirely upon Him" (*Grace and Glory* [New York: Morehouse-Barlow, 1961], pp. 68-69). That is the value of praise. Our praise will then rise out of a pure motive: perfected love.

Early twentieth-century hymnologist Charles Gabriel wrote in his hymn "O That Will Be Glory":

When all my labors and trials are o'er
And I am safe on that beautiful shore,
Just to be near the dear Lord I adore
Will through the ages be glory for me.

He was right, except for the last line—it will be glory for *God*. In fact, our greatest joy will be giving glory to God.

We will adore God forever with all our creative energies—through our thoughts, words, and song. We will express ourselves in praise through collective means and through intimate and personal means. We will praise God in every way that is possible for perfect bodies and souls.

2. Reign

In addition to worship, I believe Scripture clearly teaches that we will reign with Christ, having oversight in the operation of the eternal state.

a) A delegated reign

In this life every Christian has been given certain responsibilities within the church. Each one of us has received a spiritual gift from God that is to be used for the common good (1 Cor. 12; Rom. 12; Eph. 4). God will operate His kingdom in heaven much the same way He operates His kingdom here: delegating its operation to His people. Forever there will be a sphere of responsibility and authority.

102

b) A perfect reign

In heaven we will never fail to meet our responsibilities. In contrast Peter—who was continually given responsibilities—continually failed. He finally wanted to leave the ministry, partly because he couldn't stand his own failure. He was told to wait for the resurrected Christ in Galilee, but he decided to go fishing instead (John 21:3). I believe Peter was returning to his old trade, tired of being unable to accomplish what the Lord had delegated to him. Happily things soon turned around for him. But in heaven, we will never have to face failure.

I live with self-imposed pressure and God-imposed pressure. Although I experience false guilt for not measuring up to my self-imposed pressure, I also experience real guilt because I don't measure up to what God expects. I often have the lingering feeling that I'm wasting time and energy regardless of how much I do. Being called to serve Christ in this world is a precious opportunity I want to make the most of, so I chasten myself when I don't make the best use of my time. I look forward to the day when I will do perfectly everything the Lord gives me to do!

c) A promised reign

First Peter 1:3-4 says, "Blessed be the God and Father of our Lord Jesus Christ, who according to His great mercy has caused us to be born again to a living hope through the resurrection of Jesus Christ from the dead, to obtain an inheritance which is imperishable and undefiled and will not fade away, reserved in heaven for you." We have an inheritance in heaven right now. It's reserved for us and will never fade away. It's imperishable. And it's ours!

An inheritance is something you receive from someone else. In the Jewish context the inheritance is a sphere of responsibility or rule that a father bequeaths to his children. As we have seen in our previous studies, our inheritance includes eternal life, heaven, holiness, joy, peace, and the presence of God. In addition, Romans 8:17 says that we are "fellow heirs with Christ." However, Christ wasn't an heir to eternal life—He already had eternal life. Similarly, He already had joy, peace, and holiness. The essence of Christ's inheritance is that He is heir to this world—a sphere of rule. In Psalm 2:8 the Father tells the Son, "Ask of Me, and I will surely give the nations as Thine inheritance." Christ's inheritance is a sphere of authority over nations, demons, and the holy angels. The phrase "fellow heirs with Christ" emphasizes that we share Christ's rule over the earth.

In Revelation 5:1-3 John says, "I saw in the right hand of Him who sat on the throne a book written inside and on the back, sealed up with seven seals. And I saw a strong angel proclaiming with a loud voice, 'Who is worthy to open the book and to break its seals?' And no one in heaven, or on the earth, or under the earth, was able to open the book, or to look into it." That book is the title deed to the earth. When someone wrote a will in New Testament times, often he would roll it up seven times, putting a seal after each turn. To read the will you had to break all seven seals.

In Revelation 5:4-5 John continues, "I began to weep greatly, because no one was found worthy to open the [scroll], or to look into it; and one of the elders said to me, 'Stop weeping; behold, the Lion that is from the tribe of Judah, the Root of David, has overcome so as to open the book and its seven seals.' "

Christ alone has the right to break the seven seals. The unfolding judgments that follow depict Christ's progressive unfolding of the title deed to the earth. We will reign with Christ over the earth. I do not know what each of our specific duties will be, but we will have authority. Speaking about those who will be in heaven, Revelation 22:5 says, "They shall not have need of the light of a lamp nor the light of the sun, because the Lord God shall illumine them; and they shall reign forever and ever."

First Corinthians 6:3 adds that "we shall judge angels." We will have authority and responsibility over angels. In Matthew 19:28 Jesus says, "Truly I say to you, that you who have followed Me, in the regeneration [the rebirth of the kingdom] when the Son of Man will sit on His glorious throne, you also shall sit upon twelve thrones, judging the twelve tribes of Israel." Christ tells the apostles that they will reign over the twelve tribes of Israel—they already have their duty specified. He tells the rest of us that we have an inheritance, a sphere where we will co-reign with Christ forever.

d) A proportionate reign

Beginning in Matthew 25:14, Christ tells the parable of a man who went on a journey and left five talents to one servant, two to another, and one to the last. When the master returned, he found that the slave with five talents had made five more talents, the slave with two had made two more, and the slave with one had hidden his and only had the one talent to return. To the one with ten talents he said, "Well done, good and faithful slave; you were faithful with a few things, I will put you in charge of many things, enter into the joy of your master" (v. 21). I believe that is a picture of heaven for the faithful person who made the most of his spiritual gifts by serving others. The more faithful you are in this life, the more responsibility you will be given in the life to come. Somehow our rule in heaven is proportionate to our faithfulness in this life.

Some may wonder why any distinction should be made between the one who received five and the one who received two—they both doubled what they had been given. God is equitable and just, but He is also sovereign. And in this life He has chosen to give gifts to some that will allow them to minister to more people than others. In eternity God will exercise His sovereign purpose in the same way. We will have differing responsibilities. But no one will be jealous, boastful, or envious because we will all be perfect. We have unequal opportunity here.

Some people heard the gospel when they were young and walked with Christ for years. Others came to Christ a week before they died. Someone could ask, "Was God fair to let that person live his whole life in sin and corruption before saving him?" But God is sovereign and has the right to do what He chooses. The potter does what He wants, and the clay has no right to ask questions.

None of us will rule over a tribe of Israel, but the apostles will. It isn't a question of better or worse; it's a question of God's design for us. We all have different capacities, and God will use those capacities according to His predetermined plan. In heaven you will be the fulfillment of everything God intended for you. The U.S. Army advertises, "Be all that you can be." But the army cannot make you all that you can be; only God can do that. And someday in heaven He will.

I believe the parable of the talents depicts heaven, because when the Lord confronted the slave with one talent, He said, "Cast out the worthless slave into the outer darkness" (v. 30)—a picture of hell. The contrast is that one slave is in hell and the other two are in heaven. The Lord portrays heaven as a place where we will share His joy and reign with Him.

In Luke 19 Christ says, "A certain nobleman went to a distant country . . . and he called ten of his slaves and gave them ten minas" (v. 12-13). Verses 15-16 say, "It came about that when he returned, after receiving the kingdom, he ordered that these slaves, to whom he had given the money, be called to him in order that he might know what business they had done. And the first appeared, saying, 'Master, your mina has made ten minas more.' " That slave responded to God's call and made the most of his spiritual opportunity.

The master said to him, " 'Well done, good slave, because you have been faithful in a very little thing, be in authority over ten cities.' And the second came, saying, 'Your mina, Master, has made five minas.' And he said to him also, 'And you are to be over five cities' " (vv. 17-19). We will have authority in heaven.

In Revelation 3:20-21 Christ tells the Laodicean church, "Behold, I stand at the door and knock; if anyone hears My voice and opens the door, I will come in to him, and will dine with him, and he with Me. He who overcomes [i.e., a believer; 1 John 5:4-5], I will grant to him to sit down with Me on My throne, as I also overcame and sat down with My Father on His throne." The Bible stresses our ruling in heaven.

Conclusion

In heaven we will not spend our time sitting on the edge of a cloud and playing a harp, or in strolling golden streets, or in picking flowers in a massive celestial garden. We will be busier than we have ever been, yet will do perfect work and never grow tired. We will each fulfill the inheritance God has given us and yet rest at the same time. God has built into human nature a drive to accomplish a goal and objective. One of life's greatest pleasures is satisfaction over a job well done. In heaven we will be able to smile in the presence of God, knowing that each task in the sphere of our delegated authority will be executed perfectly. That will be a small part of the praise we will offer to God.

The measure of our responsibility in heaven will be related to the measure and use of our giftedness on earth. How we live right now dictates how we will serve in eternity. Be sure you make the most of your spiritual privileges, and reap the benefits both now and later.

Focusing on the Facts

1. Explain what we will not do in heaven (see p. 97).
2. What is the essence of heaven (see p. 97)?

3. What was God's purpose in salvation? Support your answer with Scripture (see p. 98).
4. Explain the problems we have praising God on earth (see p. 98).
5. Explain the meaning of Revelation 14:6-7 (see pp. 98-99).
6. What passages in Revelation establish the importance of praise in heaven? Explain each (see pp. 98-101).
7. What will be the motive of our praise in heaven (see p. 102)?
8. In what way will God's heavenly kingdom be like His kingdom now (see p. 102)?
9. Christ is an heir to what (see p. 104)?
10. What is "the book" in Revelation 5:1-3 (see p. 104)?
11. What will be the apostles' duty in heaven (Matt. 19:28; see p. 105)?
12. What does the parable of the talents teach us about heaven (see pp. 105-7)?
13. Who is "the overcomer" in Revelation 3:20-21 (see p. 107)?

Pondering the Principles

1. Although the Bible doesn't tell us everything about heaven, what it does tell us should elicit unending praise. When we consider what we were apart from Christ and what we will enjoy in heaven because of Him, our lives should be one mighty chorus of praise. Take time now to express to God how thankful and full of praise you are because of the place He is preparing for you. Ask Him for a greater awareness of the fleeting value of this world and the surpassing value of the world to come. Begin now to do what we will do perfectly in heaven: praising God.

2. It is sobering to realize that our opportunities in heaven are related to our faithfulness on earth. Every Christian has the duty to minister to his family, fellow believers, needy people, and unbelieving friends and acquaintances. How faithful have you been in fulfilling that responsibility? Have you allowed trivial things to preoccupy your mind, time, and energies? Is it your love for God and an awareness of His love that compels you, or is it something else? Set aside some time today to reflect on your service for Christ and earnestly ask Him to help you make the best use of your time on earth.

8
Looking Toward Heaven—Part 8
What We Will Do—Part 2

Outline

Review
I. What Heaven Is
II. Where Heaven Is
III. What Heaven Is Like
IV. What We Will Be Like
V. How We Will Relate to One Another
VI. How We Will Relate to God
VII. What We Will Do
    A. Worship
    B. Reign

Lesson
    C. Serve
        1. Heavenly service depicted
            a) The imagery of priestly service
            b) The illustrations of priestly service
        2. Earthly service rewarded
            a) Summarized
            b) Specified
    D. Rest
    E. Be Served

Conclusion

Review

I. WHAT HEAVEN IS (see pp. 13-20)

II. WHERE HEAVEN IS (see pp. 28-30)

III. WHAT HEAVEN IS LIKE (see pp. 30-53)

IV. WHAT WE WILL BE LIKE (see pp. 58-68)

V. HOW WE WILL RELATE TO ONE ANOTHER (see pp. 73-83)

VI. HOW WE WILL RELATE TO GOD (see pp. 86-92)

VII. WHAT WE WILL DO

A. Worship (see pp. 98-102)

B. Reign (see pp. 102-7)

Lesson

C. Serve

1. Heavenly service depicted

   a) The imagery of priestly service

   We will have duties to perform in heaven. In Revelation 1:6 John says, "He has made us to be a kingdom, priests to His God and Father." What do priests do? They serve God. Hannah dedicated her child, Samuel, to the Lord by taking him to the high priest and leaving him to serve at the house of God. The keynote of the priesthood was intimate service.

   In the Old Testament we read that the priest had a unique relationship to God. In fact, no common Israelite could go near anything that symbolized the presence of God. Only the descendants of Levi could serve at the Tabernacle, and out of them only

110

the descendants of Aaron could serve as priests. Numbers 16 shows how serious this exclusionary service was. Korah, Dathan, and Abiram were Levites. They were not descendants of Aaron, but they nevertheless insisted on being priests, defying Moses. They and their families experienced terrible judgment as a result. The priesthood was indeed exclusive. Only the high priest could enter the Holy of Holies—and then only once a year.

When Jesus Christ died on the cross, the veil of the Temple was rent from top to bottom; the Holy of Holies was exposed to everyone (Matt. 27:51). By graphic illustration God was saying that all who believe in Christ could enter His presence. Therefore, in the New Covenant every believer is a priest—we all have access to God. Peter calls us a royal priesthood (1 Pet. 2:9) because we are kings and priests.

First Peter 2:9 adds that we have been called "out of darkness into His marvelous light." To the Jewish reader that pictured walking into the Shekinah, the consuming presence of God. But now since Christ has made our way open, we can enter God's marvelous light. That is because we are "a people for God's own possession" (1 Pet. 2:9). Under the New Covenant every believer enjoys intimacy and access to God. That's why the writer of Hebrews said, "Let us therefore draw near with confidence to the throne of grace" (Heb. 4:16). We boldly enter God's presence to commune with Him, and out of that intimate communion we serve Him. There's no priesthood, no human intermediary, between us and God. Paul said, "There is one God, and one mediator also between God and men . . . Christ Jesus" (1 Tim. 2:5).

In heaven we will serve as perfect priests, approaching not only the throne of grace but also the throne of glory. Now we can go no farther than the throne of grace. If we approached the throne of glory, we would be consumed because of our sin. Revelation 21:3 says that in heaven God will dwell among us, and we will be His people. We will never need to cleanse ourselves by washing at a laver. We will never need to offer sacrifices. All that was completed in the past.

Isaiah 58:13-14 says, "If because of the sabbath, you turn your foot from doing your own pleasure on My holy day, and call the sabbath a delight, the holy day of the Lord honorable, and shall honor it, desisting from your own ways, from seeking your own pleasure, and speaking your own word, then you will take delight in the Lord, and I will make you ride on the heights of the earth; and I will feed you with the heritage of Jacob your father, for the mouth of the Lord has spoken." God has always wanted those who represent Him to delight in serving Him. And that is exactly what will happen in heaven. We will turn completely from our own pleasure and will call the Sabbath rest of eternity a delight. Therefore He will make us to ride the heights. The Sabbath of heaven is indeed a rest, but it is not a rest of idleness: it is unwearied, unweakened, undistracted service of God.

b) The illustrations of priestly service

In Revelation 7 John says, "Behold, a great multitude, which no one could count, from every nation and all tribes and peoples and tongues, standing before the throne and before the Lamb, clothed in white robes, and palm branches were in their hands; and they cry out with a loud voice, saying, 'Salvation to our God who sits on the throne, and to the Lamb.' And all the angels were standing around the throne, and around the elders and the four living creatures; and they fell on their faces before the throne and worshiped God, saying, 'Amen, blessing and glory and wisdom and thanksgiving and honor and power and might, be to our God forever and ever, Amen.' And one of the elders answered, saying to me, 'These who are clothed in the white robes, who are they, and from where have they come?' And I said to him, 'My lord, you know.' And he said to me, 'These are the ones who come out of the great tribulation, and they have washed their

112

robes and made them white in the blood of the Lamb' " (vv. 9-14).

The great multitude are the ones redeemed during the tribulation period, the seven-year period of judgment on the earth after the rapture of the church. The text continues, "For this reason, they are before the throne of God. And they serve Him day and night in His temple; and He who sits on the throne shall spread His tabernacle [tent] over them. They shall hunger no more, neither thirst anymore; neither shall the sun beat down on them, nor any heat; for the Lamb in the center of the throne shall be their shepherd, and shall guide them to springs of the water of life; and God shall wipe every tear from their eyes" (vv. 15-17). No tears, exhaustion, heat, hunger, or thirst will be present in heaven. We will be in the presence of the Lamb, who is our shepherd and our guide, serving as intimate priests. God will spread his tabernacle over us—we will never be out of His presence. And the Lamb is at the center of everything. The Greek word translated "serve" (la-treuō) speaks of the service a priest renders to God.

In heaven we will not serve each other; we will serve God. We will not need to strengthen each other's weaknesses because we will all be perfect and like Christ. Revelation 22 says, "He showed me a river of the water of life, clear as crystal, coming from the throne of God and of the Lamb, in the middle of its street. And on either side of the river was the tree of life, bearing twelve kinds of fruit, yielding its fruit every month; and the leaves of the tree were for the healing of the nations. And there shall no longer be any curse; and the throne of God and of the Lamb shall be in it, and His bond-servants shall serve Him; and they shall see His face, and His name shall be on their foreheads. And there shall no longer be any night; and they shall not have need of the light of a lamp nor the light of the sun, because the Lord God shall illumine them; and they shall reign forever and ever" (vv. 1-5). We will reign forever. We will serve as priests forever.

Although we do not know the specifics, we will serve God in some way. God has built into man a creative drive to accomplish something productive. We derive pleasure from a job well done and from knowing that others are pleased with our service. How wonderful to serve God in a way that pleases Him! We will have the challenge of accomplishing something—and accomplishing it perfectly. And God won't make it automatically perfect; you'll do it yourself.

2. Earthly service rewarded

a) Summarized

I believe that our service here on earth determines the nature of our service in heaven. The service you will render then is directly proportional to how well you apply yourself here. That is your reward. Believers' rewards aren't something you wear on your head like a crown, stripes on your white robe, more rooms in your mansion, or a bigger and faster chariot to drive. Your reward in heaven will be your capacity of service. The greater your commitment to service on earth, the greater will be your capacity for service in heaven. First Corinthians 4:5 says, "Do not go on passing judgment before the time, but wait until the Lord comes who will both bring to light the things hidden in the darkness and disclose the motives of men's hearts; and then each man's praise will come to him from God." When the Lord returns, each man will receive praise from God— and from God alone. To Paul no person's judgment of him mattered, not even his own (v. 3), because even if he wasn't aware of any guilt, that didn't mean he was innocent. He knew the day would come when God would judge his motives and service and would reward Him. Likewise, God plans to reward every believer. Notice that Paul said, "Each man's praise will come to him" (v. 5). Every believer will receive a reward.

First Corinthians 3:12 says, "If any man builds upon the foundation [of Christ] with gold, silver, precious stones, wood, hay, straw, each man's work will be-

114

come evident." We will all be rewarded, but each will be rewarded differently based on the value of his service. Some works will be the value of gold, silver, and precious stones. Others will be more on the level of wood, hay, and straw. Wood, hay, and straw are not evil; they just are not as valuable or durable. Therefore, our reward will be the capacity with which we will be allowed to serve God in glory.

b) Specified

Scripture has much to say about rewards. Daniel 12:3 says, "Those who have insight will shine brightly like the brightness of the expanse of heaven, and those who lead the many to righteousness, like the stars forever and ever." Daniel is saying that the basis of our reward is our faithfulness in proclaiming righteousness. And the wisdom we manifest in this life will determine how we shine in eternity.

In 1 Thessalonians 2:19-20 Paul says, "Who is our hope or joy or crown of exaltation? Is it not even you, in the presence of our Lord Jesus at His coming? For you are our glory and joy." Part of our reward in heaven will be the joy of seeing those who are there because of our faithfulness.

In 1 Corinthians 9:25 Paul says, "Everyone who competes in the games exercises self-control in all things. They then do it to receive a perishable wreath, but we an imperishable." Our reward will never diminish in value or die. In 2 Timothy 4:8 Paul writes, "In the future there is laid up for me the crown of righteousness, which the Lord, the righteous Judge, will award to me on that day; and not only to me, but also to all who have loved His appearing." The "crown of righteousness" is eternal righteousness. The "crown of life" is eternal life. The "crown of joy" is eternal joy. Heaven's crowns aren't something we will wear; they are what we will experience: eternal life, eternal joy, eternal service, and eternal blessedness.

First Peter 5:2-4 says, "Shepherd the flock of God among you, exercising oversight not under compulsion, but voluntarily, according to the will of God; and not for sordid gain, but with eagerness; nor yet as lording it over those allotted to your charge, but proving to be examples to the flock. And when the Chief Shepherd appears, you will receive the unfading crown of glory." Just as the crown of life is eternal life and the crown of rejoicing is eternal rejoicing, the crown of glory is eternal glory.

In Revelation 22:12 the Lord says, "Behold, I am coming quickly, and My reward is with Me, to render to every man according to what he has done." Your capacity for eternal joy, eternal glory, and eternal service is related to what you are doing on earth. Are you building with gold, silver, and precious stones, or with wood, hay, and straw?

That ought to motivate us. Sometimes people who mean well tell me to slow down and do less. But all of us ought to spend ourselves here so that we can have the greatest possible capacity throughout eternity to glorify God.

D. Rest

We will rest in heaven. Hebrews 4:1 speaks of "entering His rest." Verse 9 declares, "There remains therefore a Sabbath rest for the people of God." Jesus said, "Take My yoke upon you, and learn from Me, for I am gentle and humble in heart; and you shall rest for your souls" (Matt. 11:29). One of the promises the Lord gives those who believe in His Son is that we will know rest from our labors. However, from what we have already studied, we know that rest in heaven does not refer to an absence of service or duty. Similarly, Luke 13:29 says that we will recline at a banquet table in the kingdom of God, but that does not mean we will sit around all the time. When Hebrews 3-4 speaks of rest for the people of God, it means that we will never be weary, weak, unfulfilled, or interrupted. It is a unique kind of rest.

Revelation 14:11, speaking of those who were judged in the tribulation, says, "The smoke of their torment goes up forever and ever; and they have no rest day and night." Contrast that with verse 12: "Here is the perseverance of the saints who keep the commandments of God and their faith in Jesus. And I heard a voice from heaven, saying, 'Write, "Blessed are the dead who die in the Lord from now on!"' "Yes," says the Spirit, "that they may rest from their labors, for their deeds follow with them."' '" Second Thessalonians 1:7 refers to the rest as *relief*.

That rest means that the more we serve, the more refreshed we will be. The law of entropy, which causes everything to break down, will have ceased. No debilitating forces will exist. The more we fulfill our purpose, the more we will be refreshed. You will never expend any energy, be out of breath, or slow your step.

Puritan Richard Baxter wrote an entire book on this subject, entitled *The Saints' Everlasting Rest* (London: Epworth, 1962 reprint). He said, "Rest; how sweet a word is this to mine ears! Methinks the sound doth turn to substance, and having entered at the ear, doth possess my brain; and thence decendeth down to my very heart: methinks I feel it stir and work, and that through all my parts and powers, but with a various work on my various parts. To my wearied senses and languid spirits it seems a quieting, powerful opiate; to my dulled powers it is spirit and life; to my dark eyes it is both eye-salve and a prospective; to my taste it is sweetness; to mine ears it is melody; to my hands and feet it is strength and nimbleness. Methinks I feel it digest as it proceeds, and increase my native heat and moisture; and, lying as a reviving cordial at my heart, from thence doth send forth lively spirits, which beat through all the pulses of my soul. Rest,—not as the stone that rests on the earth, nor as these clods of flesh shall rest in the grave so our beasts must rest as well as we: nor is it the satisfying of our fleshly lusts, nor such rest as the carnal world desireth: no, no; we have another kind of rest than these: rest we shall from all our labours, which were but the way and means to rest, but yet that is the smallest part. O blessed rest, where we shall never rest day or night, crying 'Holy, holy, holy, Lord God of sabbaths:' when we shall rest from, sin but not from worship; from suffering and sorrow, but not from solace! O blessed day, when I shall rest with God; when I shall rest in knowing, loving, rejoicing and praising; when my perfect soul and body together shall in these perfect things perfectly enjoy the most perfect God; when God also, who is love itself, shall perfectly love me; yea, and rest in his love to me, as I shall rest in my love to him and rejoice over me with joy and singing . . . as I shall rejoice in him!''

E. Be Served

In Luke 12:35-37 Christ says, "Be dressed in readiness, and keep your lamps alight. And be like men who are waiting for their master when he returns from the wedding feast, so that they may immediately open the door to him when he comes and knocks. Blessed are those slaves whom the master shall find on the alert when he comes; truly I say to you, that he will gird himself to serve, and have them recline at table, and will come up and wait on them." There is one other thing we will experience in heaven: being served by the Lord Jesus Christ Himself.

Jesus used the imagery of a great lord returning to his palace where His slaves are waiting. Everything is prepared. They have been faithful to their lord. When he arrives, he calls them together. Rather than resting after his long journey or retiring for the night, the lord tells the slaves to sit down and allow him to serve them because of his gratitude for their service to him and their readiness for his coming. He makes his slaves kings and prepares a feast for them. Then, astoundingly, he doesn't order other servants to serve them—he serves them himself!

We won't serve each other in heaven—the Lord Himself will serve us. When He returns and finds that we have been faithful, He will serve us forever. How could heaven have a greater reward than that? It is wonderful to think of worshiping Him forever, of reigning with Him forever, of serving Him forever, and of resting forever. Yet most incredible of all is to realize that He will serve us forever. But it should not surprise us too much. After all, He washed the disciples' feet because He loved them (John 13).

Conclusion

Puritan Thomas Watson said in his *Body of Divinity* that a true saint every day takes a turn in heaven—his thoughts and desires are like cherubim flying up to paradise. When we understand what the Bible teaches about heaven, it becomes sensible to look toward heaven and set our affections on it.

There are several benefits of looking toward heaven:

A. Looking toward heaven is evidence of genuine salvation

A preoccupation with heaven is often a good indication that you are saved. Is heaven where your heart is? Do you long to be in the heavenlies? Do you long to commune with God? Do you invest as much of your treasures in heaven as possible? Are your affections set on things above, not on earthly things? A heart set on heaven is a heart set on God. And a heart set on God is a heart God has changed. The truest evidence of saving grace may well be a heavenly attitude.

B. Looking toward heaven produces Christian character

Nothing compels us to be what God wants us to be more strongly than the truths about heaven. If you understand your inheritance and the rewards, glories, joys, and privileges of heaven, and you understand that Christ Himself will serve you forever out of gratitude for what you have done, that will compel you to excellence of character. Communing with the Lord of heaven through prayer, meditation, and devotion purges the heart and produces obedience.

C. Looking toward heaven is the truest path to joy

If you want to be miserable, focus on this world. If you want to be joyful, focus on heaven. David said that the presence of God gladdens the heart (Ps. 21:6). Paul said that the eternal weight of glory is far beyond anything we suffer now (2 Cor. 4:17).

119

D. Looking toward heaven protects us from temptation and sin

One of Satan's main temptations is to get us to focus on earthly matters. But a believer whose mind is on heaven, who longs for full righteousness and the presence of God, is not easy prey for Satan.

E. Looking toward heaven maintains the vigor of our spiritual service

If you run slowly in the Christian race, contributing little in terms of Christian service and financial giving, you obviously have little regard for the promised prize. If you properly valued the heavenly prize, it would compel you to give of yourself and your resources. Fervency springs from a vision of heaven's reward.

F. Looking toward heaven honors God before all

When your heart is set on heaven, you demonstrate your love for God. Your faithful service gives the people who see you a high view of God—they see God not only as all demanding, but as all worthy. Dwell on the heavenlies and you will honor God. Dwell on the earthly things and you will dishonor God by implying they are more valuable than He is.

G. Looking toward heaven repays God

God always sets His heart on us. Therefore it is only fair that we set our hearts on Him! There is certainly nothing in this world worthy of such attention.

David said, "I shall be satisfied, when I awake, with thy likeness" (Ps. 17:15, KJV). Will anything less than that satisfy you?

Focusing on the Facts

1. What special privilege did the priests enjoy (see pp. 110-11)?
2. Explain the significance of Matthew 27:51 (see p. 111).

3. What would be brought to the mind of an Israelite when he read 1 Peter 2:9, (see p. 111)?
4. Are there any human mediators of the New Covenant? Support your answer with Scripture (see p. 111).
5. Who are the people in white robes in Revelation 7:9? What are they doing (see pp. 112-13)?
6. Will we serve each other in heaven? Explain (see p. 113).
7. What will be a believer's actual reward? On what basis will rewards be given (see p. 114)?
8. _____ _____ will receive a reward (see p. 114).
9. What is the difference between gold, silver, and precious stones and wood, hay, and straw (1 Cor. 3:12; see p. 115)?
10. Heaven's crowns are not something we will wear; they are what we will _____ . Explain (see p. 115).
11. Define the rest we will enjoy in heaven (see pp. 116-17).
12. Explain the significance of Luke 12:35-37 (see p. 118).

Pondering on the Principles

1. Under Old Testament law only the high priest had direct access into the place that represented God's presence. The people were kept away from that place by a veil, symbolizing that God had not yet opened the way into His presence (cf. Heb. 9:7-8). But when Christ died, God ripped that veil from top to bottom, demonstrating that the way into His presence is available to all. Do you take your access to God's presence for granted? Have you grown accustomed to that privilege? Read and meditate on the truths of Hebrews 10:19-25, and thank God for the access to Him that you enjoy.

2. Take time to reread the benefits of looking toward heaven on pages 119-20. How many of those benefits were present in your life before you began this study? If several were not, perhaps your heavenly perspective had become clouded. How many of those benefits are present in your life now? Did you progress? If not, perhaps you have merely accumulated academic knowledge about heaven and have failed to apply it. Ask God to make His Word live in you. Determine that the reality of God's Word will permeate every aspect of your life.

121

Scripture Index

Topical Index